SANDRA
Keep on Cooking

1

Copyright © 2009, 2010 by Dave Martin

'Flavor Quest'
Volume Two

Chef Dave Martin gives you more of his favorite
recipes for you to continue on or begin your own
personal 'Flavor Quest'

Get More of Dave's Secrets to Salads You'll Love, Sexy
Side Kicks, Munchables, Big Dippers, Exciting Entrees,
Guilty Pleasures & Cocktails 'a' Plenty

Dedication & Acknowledgements:

This book would not have been possible without the love and support of my friends and family. My culinary adventure started as a young boy in a kitchen where my mother, grandmother and even my father shared their passion for cooking. I was spoiled by having fresh baked goodies and home cooked meals from an early age. I never realized how special that was until many years later. The recipes in this book come from my heart and I hope that you will enjoy them and share them with your good friends and family. Yes, my dedication is the same from my first book because my story has not changed and my inspiration remains the same and for that I am truly thankful.

Special thanks to:

Mom, Sis & Al, Phil, Irene & Frank, Carolyn, Sara, Dorf, Adam, Anthony, Spud, Shauna, Karen, Gina (3 of them), Stacey, Dirk, Heather, Kim, Mike, Shelley, Brad, Renee & Wyatt, Brent, Kristin, Tom, Kathy, Jamie, Valerie, Emily, Fran, Jane, Andy, Kathryn, Kerry, Annie, Melissa, Allison, Hobbit, Jan, Ed, Andrea, Donna, Thera & Alex (my editor)

'Flavor Quest'

In my first book, I encouraged you to explore your kitchens and to try new recipes to embark on your own personal food journey (quest). With this book, the same goals apply, but with a whole new set of tools/tricks from my arsenal for you to experiment with at home. I intentionally set up the Flavor Quest Series so that you would have the opportunity to mix and match various recipes and dishes that work well together. It's all about the Garanimals principle for me (if you remember the old school clothing line that helped you when you were a kid and didn't know a thing about what to wear with what. It was all about matching the zebra shirt with the zebra pants for the perfect outfit.) Think of my books as the same type of tool for the home cook, where you have dishes/flavors that work well together to create the ideal meal. My books are building blocks that while they work great independently, they have much more power working together. Volume One was the foundation and Volume Two introduces more dishes into the mix which afford you brand new options to create a menu for a large gathering or a romantic dinner for two. I am really excited about this book because it has entire sections devoted to things like side dishes, sauces and even some tasty cocktails.

I really love being able to share my tricks from the restaurant and catering world to you at home. It puts a smile on my face to receive feedback from those that currently have the first volume, so please continue to let me know about your personal triumphs with my books. It's what drives me to pursue my true passion of helping everyone to be a better cook.

And yes, I will be teasing you with menu ideas using recipes from my first book, but it's only because I truly believe that you can be an even better home cook/entertainer by having a large collection of quality recipes to back you up. Isn't that what a great series is all about?

Now that we've got that out of the way, it's time to get started and continue forward on your 'Flavor Quest', or get you started on your initial journey. Remember to never take it too seriously and have fun!

Take care and see you soon.
Dave

Introduction & Welcome:

Thank you for picking up a copy of my second cookbook. After all of the awesome feedback from my first book, I had to follow-up with more great recipes and another collection of classics and favorites. Like the first book, 95% of these recipes have been restaurant tested on both the East & West Coasts with excellent results.

In Volume Two of Flavor Quest, I really wanted to give you some more motivation in the form of new ideas & recipes so that you can continue to have a great time in the kitchen, while encouraging you to spend even more time with your good friends and family.

My true reward from cooking comes from pleasing other people and I think that most people that love to cook feel the same way. I mean, I love the cooking part too, but the comments after the meal are really important to me. Cooking is all about taking time out of your day and your life to make other people happy and there really is no feeling like it in the world.

This past year has been such a crazy year for me- full of fantastic adventures and surprises. I was at a real crossroads when I put together my last book, and although I knew what I wanted to do in the food world, I didn't know if I could really make it happen. I knew that I wanted to keep cooking and teaching, but not in the structured uber stressful restaurant environment full of crazy owners and more headaches than you can imagine. I also had a real desire to reach out and to help others in need and specifically kids in need. I began by calling Corporate Headquarters for the Make-A-Wish Foundation and asking, 'How can I Help?' Ironically at the same time, other organizations began contacting me to be a part of their fundraising efforts which began a series of successful partnerships. It is amazing as I think about it now and I am so grateful to be able to help and to give back. Who would have thought that I could help raise money and awareness by sharing my passion for food and cooking? Life is good.

When I left the traditional restaurant world behind last year, I decided to try to make it all happen on my own. I started contacting winemakers and cooking schools along with some of my favorite brands. Through my grass roots cold calling and marketing efforts, I began booking more events and gigs for myself. I took on the role of PR/Agent/Author and Marketing Manager all at the same time, with some amazing results. I've only just begun my Quest and pursuit of my passion and of my love for food (eating, cooking, teaching, and sharing).

Introduction & Welcome, continued:

I am truly doing what I love which is sharing my love of food and wine with folks from around the country. I've been teaching classes and doing cooking demonstrations in several states with many more to follow (so if you have any ideas/locations, please let me know via facebook or twitter).

I really want to thank all of you that have embraced me and helped me to continue my personal journey (Flavor Quest). I wouldn't be able to do it without so much help and support from everyone and may I inspire you all to pursue yours as well. Thank You.

CONTENTS

Salads You'll Love...21

'Crave' House Salad- lemon vinaigrette & roasted mushrooms
Salad of Duck Confit-apple cider vinaigrette, oven roasted pears, crispy potato pancake and duck confit
Roasted Beet Salad –sherry vinaigrette & nutmeg walnuts
Watermelon Salad-basil, mint and goats cheese
Roasted Veggie Orzo Salad

Side Kicks...37

Toasted Coconut Rice
Currant, Cilantro & Almond Cous Cous
Parsnip & Roasted Garlic Puree
Triple Olive Tapenade
Sweet & Sour Pickles
House Made Guac'
Apple Wood Bacon Refried Black Beans
Queso Fundido

Munchables...49

Pan Roasted Mussels-smoked paprika aioli
Citrus Marinated Flank Steak
Lamb Meatballs
Pan Fried Shrimp & Veggie Dumplings-tangy soy sauce
Vietnamese Style Spring Rolls-nuoc cham
Goat Cheese & Green Apple Ravioli
Free Range Chicken Tenders-chipotle glaze & how, now- kung pao sauce
Salt & Brown Sugar Cured Salmon

The Big Dippers...73

Dave's Peanut Sauce
Walnut & Basil Pesto

Tangy Shallot, White Wine & Mustard Sauce
Tzatziki Sauce
Roasted Tomato Salsa
Spicy Sweet Honey Mustard
Sweet Onion & Apple Compote

Entrees, Burgers & More, Oh my...83

Coca Cola Braised Beef Short Ribs- smokey rub
Maple & Thyme Roasted Turkey- turkey pan gravy
Apple Mango Free Range Chicken-peach & plum salsa
Hoisin & Cider Lamb Chops & Pork Satay- marinade for lamb and
pork, mango & apricot chutney
Wild Striped Bass with Roasted Garlic Butter & Veggies
Stuffed Pork Tenderloin
Ground Chicken Burger
Tasty Turkey Burger

Guilty Pleasures...103

Lemon Vanilla Sponge Cake- seasonal berries & mascarpone cream
Butterscotch Pudding
Death by Cocoa Cake
Roasted Pistachio Oil & White Chocolate Biscotti
Crème Fraiche Ice Cream
Hot Fudge Sauce
Caramel Sauce
Homemade Marshmallows

More Cocktails, Please...119

Traditional Bloody Mary
Yellow Tomato Mary
Ginger Pom Martini
The 'Apple Jack'
Guava Mojito
Prickly Pear Margarita
The Brooklyn Blues

Terms, Tips & Methods:

50/50 blend- in my world, it's a blend of 50% kosher salt and 50% ground black pepper. I use it to season all of my proteins, veggies and everything else when I need basic seasoning.

Blend oil- usually a blend of canola and olive oil (a little less expensive and fine to use for starting a dish or sauce but not for finishing). I usually use EVO but if you can't afford it, you can use regular olive oil or a quality blend oil.

Caramelize- to heat until browned and cooked through. Not just sweating the liquid out, but releasing the sugars and the depth of flavor (method used for onions, shallots, veggies etc).

Chiffonade- in French-'made of rags' but in kitchen terms it refers to thin strips or shreds of herbs or vegetables

Composed salad- a salad in which the ingredients are artfully arranged versus being thrown together or tossed together in a bowl

Creaming Method- whip the butter until it is light yellow in color

Crème fraiche- a matured, thickened cream that has a slightly tangy, nutty flavor and a rich texture

Currants- a tiny dark raisin created from dried Champagne grapes

Dredge- to lightly coat in flour or a rub before cooking

Duck confit- in this case it is the preserving of duck by covering in salt and slow cooking in its own fat

Emulsify- also a binding agent or thickener. In our case, we will use pomegranate molasses and honey in the vinaigrettes to help thicken versus using excessive oil.

EVO or EVOO- Extra Virgin Olive Oil

Fresh juices- in all of these recipes when calling for orange, lemon or lime juice, please use fresh squeezed only. I cannot stand by the flavor that will be produced by a bottled product.

Frisee- a member of the chicory family, it's like a feathery lettuce with curly leaves that are yellowish-white to green and is mildly bitter. A nice mix with simple mixed greens.

Hatch chiles- an area in New Mexico that grows some of the best chiles in the world, the chiles come in different heat levels from mild (New Mexico) to extra-hot (Barker)

Heirloom- fruits and vegetables that are grown from 'heirloom' seeds that have been open-pollinated and not coming from the produce-seed mega companies. Think of

Heirloom, continued:
heirloom as precisely the true meaning of the word like an old piece of jewelry or something handed down by the generations (in this case coming from Mother Nature's jewelry box and not the science lab).

Immersion blender- a hand held blender that can be used to blend soups or sauces by placing into the liquid. It's okay if you don't have one: simply use your food processor or table top blender as needed, but place a rag over the top if you are working with a heated liquid so you don't burn you or anyone else.

Julienne- to cut food into thin, matchstick or thin strips

Kosher salt-the only salt used throughout this entire cookbook for its balanced flavor. Do not used iodized or Morton salt. Sea/Grey and other salts may be too bold for the recipes in this book, so scale back if using them.

Lardons- narrow strips of bacon or fat that are diced and cooked or fried

Mandoline- a cooking utensil used for slicing and for cutting firm vegetables and fruits. It consists of two parallel working surfaces, one of which can be adjusted in height. A food item is slid along the adjustable surface until it reaches a blade mounted on the fixed surface, slicing it and letting it fall. Other blades perpendicular to the main blade are often mounted so that the slice is cut into strips. It also makes slices, waffle cuts and crinkle cuts.

Mirepoix- a mixture of diced carrots, celery and onions used to season soups, sauces, and stews as well as provide a bed to braise meats on.

Mirin- a low-alcohol wine made from rice, which adds sweetness and flavor to Asian dishes.

Napa Cabbage- a Chinese Cabbage whose flavor has been described by some as delicate compared to bok choy or regular cabbage. It can be used in stir-fry with other ingredients such as tofu, mushrooms or zucchini to give you more texture and crunch.

Nappe- refers to either the ability of a liquid to "coat the back of a spoon" or the act of coating a food (i.e. to nappe a leg of lamb with glaze).

Non-reactive bowl- a non-reactive bowl is a bowl made of a substance that won't react chemically with the foods you place in it. Reactive bowls are often made of metal or plastics that stain easily. Typical reactive metals include copper, cast iron and aluminum. When you add any high acid foods to these bowls — like lemon juice, most citrus fruits or tomato sauce — they may actually react with the metal in the bowls and impart a metallic taste to your foods. If you're looking for a non-reactive bowl made of metal, you always want to look for stainless steel, since it tends to resist reaction with high acid foods.

Nuoc Cham- a Vietnamese fish sauce with chiles, garlic, lime juice, ginger and sugar.

Orzo- barley in Italian; tiny rice shaped pasta used in soups.

Paint- using a pastry brush, paint butter or oil onto a biscuit, ear of corn or pie dough.

Parsnip- a root vegetable (white in color), kind of like a carrot in appearance and usually used like you would a potato in purees or mashed form; but of course you can roast them as well.

Pastry brush- a small brush used for applying glazes to baked goods. Usually nylon and now there are silicone varieties available that work quite nicely and don't leave hairs behind.

'PEI 'Mussels- Prince Edward Island, a Canadian Province known for its harbors and caves where some of the tastiest mussels are harvested and shipped to us here in the U.S.

Pinch- unless you have giant fingers this should be about a $\frac{1}{2}$ teaspoon.

Pomegranate molasses- a thick, syrupy pomegranate juice reduction that is tart and slightly sweet at the same time.

Queso fundido- Spanish for 'melted cheese'; a south of the border fondue usually containing chorizo, Jack cheese, onions, garlic and tomatoes.

Roasted garlic/shallots- this is used in many of my recipes. Method: On the stove, heat 10 peeled garlic cloves and about 1-2 tsp of olive oil on medium to low heat for about 5-10 minutes. It's quick and easy. Increase accordingly based on how much you need, and you can also roast off a large batch and store covered in your fridge for a couple of weeks. Roast off the larger quantities in the oven at 350 degrees for 30-40 minutes or until heavily browned in a skillet or on a baking sheet.

Roasting method- what I use for all vegetables and my garlic. Use EVO, kosher salt and black pepper and cook at 350 degrees until the veggies are cooked but still have some crunch.

Rondeau- large pan used for braising (long slow cooking method)

Sauté- to jump in the pan (French) using little oil or fat using high heat and to rapidly brown meat or veggie

Sherry wine- a fortified wine traditionally made in Spain that makes everything taste better (you will see this in just about every one of my sauce recipes). The flavor of sherry is unique but you can use dry, golden, fino or cream- the flavors differ but any of them will work.

Smoked paprika- the peppers are slow roasted over oak providing a wonderful smoky taste. You can use Hungarian or Spanish but the flavor will not match the smoked version.

Straw mushrooms- a mushroom that is actually grown on straw that's been used in a paddy. They have a musty, earthy flavor and are about 1 inch in size.

Sweat- gentle heat and a little oil, to remove moisture without adding color to the veggies.

Sweet onions- other names include Vidalia, Walla Walla, and Maui. These onions are sweeter and have a better flavor to me. I do not use brown, yellow or white onions in my kitchen, it's simply a preference. You are welcome to use what is available to you, but go with brown or yellow before white, if possible.

Water Bath- to surround food by water while in a pan or baking dish. Primarily used for baking custards, and to help cheesecakes from curdling or over-baking, thus producing a creamier end product.

Zest- the perfumy outermost colored skin layer of citrus fruit which adds aromatic oils and flavors to food.

Oven Times and Temperatures:
While these recipes have been tested thoroughly and used in restaurant production, every oven is different. Some are not calibrated properly and cook at higher or lower heats. If you cook at home, you may already know your ovens strengths and weaknesses. So with that said, keep an eye on your timing when tackling the recipe for the first time to ensure that it works out on your end.

Resources:
For measurement questions or conversions go to:
http://www.ez-calculators.com

Where to Buy/Partners & Friends:

The Perfect Puree of Napa Valley- Specialty Purees and Premium Mixers
http://www.perfectpuree.com

La Tourangelle- Handcrafted Gourmet Oils (hazelnut, pumpkin, etc)
http://www.latourangelle.com

Certified Angus Beef Brand- It is the original brand of fresh beef, brought to you by farmers and ranchers across America
http://www.certifiedangusbeef.com

Culinary Vegetable Institute & The Chefs Garden-
Pioneers in Specialty Vegetables & Sustainable Agriculture
http://www.culinaryvegetableinstitute.com
http://www.chefsgarden.com

Crocs- Killer Footwear
http://www.crocs.com

New Chef Fashion, Inc. - Chef Wear & Accessories
http://www.newchef.com

D'Artagnan- Natural and Organic Fresh Meats, Foie Gras, Truffles & Gourmet Products
http://www.dartagnan.com

Nueske's- America's Original Apple wood Smoked Meats
http://www.nueskes.com

La Espanola Meats- Creators of Charcuterie & Purveyors of Fine Foods from Spain
http://www.lasespanolameats.com

Salads You'll Love...

'Salads You'll Love' is just that- a group of fun salads great for any small dinner party or group gathering. I love putting together tasty salads, and with this new collection of flavors and ingredients, you really can't go wrong.

Salads can be a great way to get things started, like my Crave House Salad, which is a light but flavorful salad from my days at 'Crave on 42nd'. This simple salad with roasted mushrooms, parmesan and fresh lemon vinaigrette really wakes you up with the bold tang of the fresh lemon.

The Salad of Duck Confit could actually be served as a meal itself- it has protein, starch, greens & some yummy flavors that really work well together. This salad has a lot of components so if you are feeling overwhelmed then you can serve just the duck, greens and vinaigrette.

Now, let's talk about beets. You *must* make the Roasted Beet Salad because it's not only beautiful, but will make a non-beet lover convert to the other side. The roasting of the beets really works to bring out the color and true flavor of the beet without being pickled and canned. I love the crunch of the Nutmeg Walnuts with the creamy cheese, roasted beets and Sherry Vinaigrette. You can see this salad on the back cover of the book.

I think both the Watermelon Salad and Roasted Veggie Orzo Salad are super alternatives to the heavy, fatty mayonnaise laden potato and macaroni salads brought to cook-outs, potlucks & BBQ's during the summer. It's just nice to have other options and that's what my cookbooks are all about, lots of new ideas and options for the home cook. So no matter how you use them, you will come to enjoy these delicious Salads You'll Love.

'Crave' House Salad
Yields 6-8 salads

**I kept the 'Crave' in the name since this was the house salad I created for my long deceased restaurant, 'Crave on 42nd in NYC. It's a really simple and yummy salad that's a great start to any meal.

Ingredients:
4-5 oz mixed greens
2 cups roasted mushrooms (pg. 23)
4-6 oz lemon vinaigrette (see below)
4 oz shaved Parmesan cheese

Method:
Wash your greens if they are not pre-washed and set aside. You can serve this in a plate or salad bowl, it's your choice. Dress your greens and mushrooms together in a medium sized mixing bowl and then after plating, top it all off with some nice large shavings of Parmesan cheese. Simple and easy to prepare and enjoy.

Lemon Vinaigrette (for 'Crave' House Salad)
Yields about 2 cups of vinaigrette

Ingredients:
1 cup fresh lemon juice
$\frac{1}{4}$ cup roasted garlic
$\frac{1}{4}$ cup extra virgin olive oil
$\frac{1}{4}$ cup honey
$\frac{1}{4}$ Tbsp deli mustard
$\frac{1}{2}$ oz chopped chives
$\frac{1}{4}$ Tbsp 50/50 blend of salt and pepper (see Terms, Tips & Methods pg.13)

Lemon Vinaigrette, continued:

Method:
Blend all ingredients together using an immersion blender or food processor. Store in the fridge for service.

Roasted Mushrooms
Yields about 2- 3 cups of roasted mushrooms

Ingredients:
4 cups of cremini mushrooms with stems, thinly sliced
2 Tbsp of EVO
1 -2 Tbsp kosher salt
2 tsp black pepper

Method:
Cook mushrooms in a pre-heated oven at 350 degrees. Drizzle mushrooms with EVO, salt, pepper and mix all ingredients together on a sheet pan/baking sheet. Bake until mushrooms are caramelized/browned for about 10-15 minutes. Remove and or to top off the 'Crave' House Salad or add to veggie medley for the Wild Striped Bass

Salad of Duck Confit
Yields about 6-8 salads

Ingredients:
12-16 oz Duck Confit (see recipe on pg. 27 or you can order prepared from Dartagnan.com)
6-8 oz Roquefort cheese, crumbled
2 each roasted pears (pg. 25)
4-5 oz frisee
6- 8 crispy potato cakes (pg.26)

Method:
This is another composed salad that takes some time in plating; but don't all fantastic salads take a little bit of time if they are worth it? I like to use a plate for this salad and I start by setting down the crispy potato cake (off to the side or center of the plate) and top if off with the warm or room temperature duck confit. Dress the rinsed frisee & pears together gently in a mixing bowl along with the Roquefort & cider vinaigrette and then snuggle the mixture up right next to the potato/duck combo. Work with plating it the way that you like best and get ready to enjoy some incredible flavor combinations.

Apple Cider Vinaigrette (for salad of duck confit)
Yields 4 cups of vinaigrette

Ingredients:
10 oz Apple Cider Vinegar
20 oz Fresh Apple Cider (you can use Martinelli's if you can't find fresh cider or other premium apple juice)
2 oz Walnut Oil
3 oz Maple Syrup, the real stuff

Apple Cider Vinaigrette, continued:

$\frac{1}{2}$ tsp Ground Cinnamon
$\frac{1}{2}$ tsp Kosher Salt
$\frac{1}{2}$ tsp Black Pepper
$\frac{1}{4}$ tsp Ground Nutmeg
2 Tbsp Brown Sugar
5 oz Mango Juice

Method:
Place all ingredients into a medium sized mixing bowl and whisk until everything is well incorporated. Double check for additional salt and pepper as needed.

Oven Roasted Pears (for salad of duck confit)
Yields enough pears for 6-8 salads

Ingredients:
2 each Comice or Bosc Pears (cored & sliced $\frac{1}{4}$ inch thick)
$\frac{1}{4}$ cup Water
$\frac{1}{2}$ Tbsp Granulated Sugar
pinch of Black Pepper
pinch of Kosher Salt

1-2 Tbsp Unsalted Sweet Butter, melted (for sheet tray)

Method:
Butter sheet tray and heat oven to 350 degrees. Mix the sugar and water together and then paint each of the pear slices or soak the pear slices in the sugar/water mixture and place onto buttered sheet tray. Dust with salt and pepper. Bake for about 8-12 minutes or until pears are oven roasted. Remove from tray, let them cool and package in wax paper in

Oven Roasted Pears, continued:

layers so that they don't stick together for storage in the refrigerator.

Crispy Potato Cakes (for duck salad)
Yields about 8/ 2 oz pancakes

Ingredients:
1 lb Yukon Gold Potatoes Peeled & Grated (Do not rinse)
1 oz Unsalted Sweet Butter, melted
$\frac{1}{2}$ Tbsp Black Pepper
$\frac{1}{2}$ Tbsp Kosher Salt
1 Tbsp White vinegar

Extra Virgin Olive Oil

Method:
In a large mixing bowl, add the vinegar to the potatoes and then blend them with butter & seasonings. Lay the potato mixture out flat to about 1 inch high on a sheet tray/baking sheet. Using a ring cutter/mold or sharp knife, cut out 3 inch circles and then immediately cover with plastic wrap so that the air does not brown the potatoes. You may have to drain the potatoes a bit before you cook them, but the vinegar helps to keep them from browning along with getting them out of the air as quickly as possible.
Heat a skillet over medium heat with olive oil and then drop in your cakes to cook until they are cooked all the way through. You can smash them with a spatula during the cooking process, then remove and drain on a paper towel. Do not cook on too high of heat or all of the potatoes will not cook through, and

Crispy Potato Cakes, continued:

do not overcrowd the skillet, otherwise they won't cook properly. You can always add a little more oil as needed if you are cooking multiple batches to keep the potatoes from sticking. Add a little bit of butter to add more flavor and increase the browning, but keep an eye on the heat. These are for Salad of Duck Confit but can also be used with the Sweet Onion & Apple Compote.

Duck Confit
Yields about 12-16 oz of confit

Ingredients:
6 duck legs, moulard is best

4 Tbsp kosher salt
12 black peppercorns
$\frac{1}{2}$ tsp cinnamon
$\frac{1}{2}$ tsp allspice
$\frac{1}{2}$ tsp ground nutmeg
$\frac{1}{4}$ tsp ground cloves
4 cloves garlic, smashed
12 sprigs fresh thyme

4 cups of duck fat (which is ideal, but for home you can use a blend oil with some olive oil for flavor. If you use just canola you really won't have any flavor).

Method:
In a pyrex dish or baking pan, mix all of the salt, herbs and spices. Roll the duck in the pan and coat all sides of the legs. Arrange the duck, skin-side up, over the herbed/salt mixture and cover and refrigerate for 1-3 days. It works best if you

27

Duck Confit, continued:

put a heavy object on top of the covered duck while it cures in the fridge. The longer you cure the duck, the better, but you can cook the meat after 1 day if that's all the time you have. More time equals more flavor.

Preheat the oven to 225°F. Remove the duck from the cure and rinse in cool water. Melt the duck fat in a small saucepan if you are using it, and place the duck pieces in a single snug layer in a high-sided baking dish or ovenproof saucepan before pouring the melted fat over the duck (or the oils that you are using instead). The duck pieces should be covered by fat/oil, then place them in the oven. Cook the confit slowly at a very slow simmer, just an occasional bubble until the duck is tender and can be easily pulled from the bone, which usually takes about 2-3 hours. Remove the confit from the oven. Cool and store the duck in the fat. When you are ready to use it for snacking or the Salad of Duck Confit, remove and clean the meat off of the legs using a fork. The confit will last for at least 2 weeks in your fridge.

Roasted Beet Salad
Yields about 6-8 salads

Ingredients:
6 each sliced roasted medium sized beets (see below)
6-8 oz Gorgonzola cheese, crumbled
4 oz nutmeg walnuts (pg. 31)
10 oz sherry vinaigrette (pg. 31)
4 oz baby arugula

Method:
If the greens are not pre-washed, then wash them and spin or towel dry. Place the nuts, washed arugula, nutmeg walnuts and gorgonzola into a mixing bowl and gently mix them with the vinaigrette. Place onto the salad plate that you are using. Take the sliced roasted beets and dress them in the same bowl. Add them to the salad making sure to showcase them along with all of the other ingredients and don't hide your beets under the greens. There are several ways to plate this salad (see picture on the back of the book or on my website for the family style version). If you are plating individual salads- key word plate- I prefer small salad plates vs. bowls. I really love this salad because of the crunch of the nuts with the creaminess of the cheese along with the zing of the arugula, tang of the vinaigrette and the wonderful flavor of the roasted beets.

Roasted Beets (for beet salad)
Enough for 6-8 salads

Ingredients:
6 each medium sized beets, washed, peeled and left whole (red, gold or various colors are ideal, but work with what you have available)

Roasted Beets, continued:

Extra Virgin Olive Oil
Kosher salt
Black pepper
Aluminum foil

Method:
After peeling the beets, coat them lightly with olive oil, kosher salt and black pepper. Wrap the beets in individual foil wrappers like little packages, making sure that the whole beet is covered up. Place the packages on a sheet tray/cookie sheet in a 350 degree oven and roast them for about 1 ½ -2 hours. If the beets are super small they will roast much quicker so keep your eyes on them and adjust the timing accordingly. I have found that with medium to large sized beets, they should come out perfectly if you use the timeline above. The test is taking a sharp paring knife and testing to see if it slides right through the beet similar to the way you test potatoes. Once cooked properly, remove from the oven, leave them in the foil and allow them to cool as the steam in the foil can be very hot, so be careful. Once the beets have cooled, remove from the foil and slice them into ¼ - ½ inch slices. Sometimes the bottom of the beet gets really caramelized, so double check to make sure it doesn't taste burnt in flavor before using it in your salad.
These beets can be used for just snacking too if you don't feel like making the salad. If you never liked beets because they were always from a can, give these a try and you might change your tune.

Sherry Vinaigrette (for beet salad)
Yields about 1 ½ cups of vinaigrette

Ingredients:
¼ Tbsp Dijon mustard
2 Tbsp shallots (minced)
1 cup sherry wine vinegar
2 Tbsp extra virgin olive oil
2 Tbsp pomegranate molasses (found in Mediterranean food stores or amazon.com)
2 Tbsp sugar
¼ Tbsp 50/50 salt and pepper blend

Method:
Place all ingredients into a blender or food processor and blend until emulsified. Store in plastic or glass container in fridge for up to 1-2 weeks.

Nutmeg Walnuts (for beet salad & butterscotch pudding)
Yields 3 cups of walnuts

24 oz of walnut pieces, chopped
1 large egg white
2 Tbsp ground cinnamon
½ cup granulated sugar
½ Tbsp black pepper
½ Tbsp kosher salt

Method:
Mix egg whites, nutmeg and spices in a large bowl. Add walnuts and mix ingredients completely to coat. They should be wet but dry and not soaking in eggs or they will not cook properly.

Nutmeg Walnuts, continued:

Heat oven to 350 degrees and cook the walnuts on a sheet tray/baking sheet for about 4-5 minutes, then stir them up and let cook on other sides for another 3-5 minutes. They will dry out once they come out of the oven and rest, and will become crispy and crunchy. Be careful not to overcook and burn.

**yes, this is the same method and recipe as my cinnamon pecans from FQ, Vol. 1, but I wanted to include it for those that haven't bought the first book, yet.

PS...this recipe works great with cashews-- and that's what I would use on the butterscotch pudding or just for munching around the house.

Watermelon Salad
Yields 6-8 salads

Ingredients:
12 oz red watermelon or yellow watermelon, small dice
12 oz red tomato or yellow tomato, small dice (or heirloom tomatoes)
*the key here is to have the watermelon and tomatoes have contrasting colors but if you can't find the various colors, it's all still great with the red on red.

Dressing:
2 tsp extra virgin olive oil
$\frac{1}{2}$ Tbsp lime juice
1 Tbsp honey
$\frac{1}{4}$ Tsp kosher salt
$\frac{1}{4}$ Tsp black pepper

2 Tbsp basil, chiffonade
2 Tbsp mint, chiffonade
3-4 Tbsp goat cheese, crumbled

Method:
Dice the watermelon and tomatoes and set aside. You will probably have watermelon juice after the melon rests, so just discard or have as a tasty beverage. In a small mixing bowl, blend oil, lime, honey, salt & pepper and whisk away. Prepare the basil and mint at service time (to avoid browning) along with the goat cheese. Dress the melon with the dressing and add another sprinkle of salt and pepper to season the melon and tomatoes. Add the herbs and then garnish with the crumbles of goat cheese and serve immediately. I don't usually

Watermelon Salad, continued:

mix all of the goat cheese in since it gets kind of ugly and works better as a garnish to the salad.

If you are prepping the salad ahead of time, just keep all of the ingredients separate until you are ready to serve. This salad works great as a lighter and healthier alternative to a potato salad at a BBQ or other summer gathering.

Roasted Veggie Orzo Salad
Yields about 8 cups of orzo/enough for about 8-12 guests

Ingredients:
1 lb Orzo
1 gallon of veggie stock
2-3 Tbsp olive oil added to the stock
2 Tbsp kosher salt

Extra Virgin Olive Oil

Method:
Rinse orzo in water and bring veggie stock water to boil. Once boiling, add the orzo, oil & salt and cook for about 8 minutes until almost cooked through. Drain and rinse in COLD water. Blend with a little bit of olive oil to keep it from sticking together and spread it out on a sheet tray/cookie sheet and then follow the steps below.

After cooking you will add the following ingredients to the orzo but feel free to have everything prepped in advance.

Ingredients:
1 cup yellow zucchini or squash, roasted (small dice)
1 cup green beans, roasted (small dice)
1 Tbsp 50/50 salt and pepper
Extra Virgin Olive Oil

$\frac{1}{2}$ bunch Italian parsley
1 cup red seedless grapes, sliced lengthwise for the shape
1 lime or lemon, juiced

Roasted Veggie Orzo Salad, continued:

Method:
Remove the tip of the green beans and slice into small dice along with the zucchini. Heat your oven to 350 degrees. Place your squash and green beans onto a sheet tray and add some olive oil, salt and pepper. Mix thoroughly with your hands so that each piece has some seasoning. Roast them off for about 5-7 minutes but don't overcook the beans or the squash. Remove from the oven and let cool for a couple of minutes. Slice your grapes lengthwise for shape and effect and then blend your roasted veggies, grapes & parsley along with the cooked and cooled orzo. Add a touch of olive oil and lime or lemon juice and adjust with additional salt and pepper, as needed. Feel free to add your other favorite seasonal veggies to this mix and make it your own. This is another great salad that can be served cool or at room temp at a party where you want a lighter, healthier option as a side dish/salad.

Side Kicks...

The Lone Ranger had Tonto, Batman had Robin, and you lucky home cooks have Me ☺ and this little roster of Sexy Side Kicks (side dishes, guest stars & companions).

The Toasted Coconut Rice and Currant, Cilantro & Almond Couscous are really nice grain options for any meal. The Toasted Coconut Rice works nicely with the Apple Mango Chicken/Peach & Plum Salsa combo or could also be fun with the Pan Fried Dumplings & Vietnamese Spring Rolls. I really love the juices with the rice along with the toasted coconut, which makes the whole dish pop.

If you've never worked with parsnips, please don't be afraid to start with my Parsnip & Roasted Garlic Puree. These root veggies are a nice change to the same old mashed potatoes you've been eating for ages. The flavor and texture of the parsnip along with the roasted garlic make this a side kick you will want to make again.

My Triple Olive Tapenade is a nice alternative to butter or olive oil for your bread at dinner. I have served this spread in restaurants on the East & West Coast with bi-coastal nods of approval.

If you have always wanted to make the perfectly balanced pickle for burgers, sandwiches or snacking, then it's time to make my easy Sweet & Sour Pickles (they have a nice shelf life in the refrigerator, too).

In putting together this second book, I realized that I hadn't shared a lot of my Mexican/Latin American recipes, so you're going to see a couple from my vast gallery of favorites (House Made Guac', Refried Black Beans, Queso Fresco, Citrus Marinated Flank Steak, Roasted Tomato Salsa & Prickly Pear Margarita). You can make all of these recipes for a Mexican Fiesta or feast at home, but all of these dishes can stand on their own as well. I'm definitely a purist when it comes to

Guacamole, so you will find that my House Made Guac' is all about the avocados and not a bunch of tomatoes, onions and other filler. It is very simple to make, but it's how I like it and I really hope that you will too. When it comes to Refried Black Beans, the ones in this chapter are done with Apple Wood Bacon Fat and they will really blow you away because they are full in flavor but actually use less fat/lard than most of the refried bean recipes out there.

Don't get me started talking about Queso Fundido because I still vividly remember sharing this dish with my good friend Jakki at the now defunct Tortilla Flats in Laguna Beach, California. The dish was so rich and tasty, but it was so oily that when I fed her a huge mouthful of it, she had cheese grease running down her entire face. I am giggling now as I recall how funny it was over some of their fantastic margaritas. But I digress, so when I created my own version of Queso Fundido, I chose cheeses and meats that have lower oil/fat contents, thus resulting in an equally tasty product but without the pools of oil.

Enjoy these Side Kicks on their own or partnered up with a supporting cast of my Munchables, Entrees or Burgers.

Toasted Coconut Rice

Yields 3 cups of cooked rice/ enough for about 6-8 portions

Ingredients:
1 cup basmati rice, rinsed
½ cup coconut milk
½ cup pineapple juice
½ cup chicken stock
1 Tbsp unsalted sweet butter
½ tsp kosher salt
2 cups toasted sweetened coconut
¾ cup red bell pepper (small dice)
¾ cup green bell pepper (small dice)

Kosher salt
Black pepper

Method:
Rinse rice in cold water to remove starch.
Place rice in rice cooker or onto stovetop in a stockpot with coconut milk, pineapple juice, chicken stock, butter and salt. Cook covered for about 15 to 20 minutes or until done over low heat if using the stovetop method vs. the rice cooker.
Small dice red & green bell peppers (¼ inch squares).
After the rice is cooked, remove from the heat and fluff it up with a fork and add in the red & green bell peppers, toasted coconut and adjust with more salt and pepper, as needed.

**Toasting Coconut-heat your oven to 350 degrees and lay your coconut out flat onto a sheet tray/cookie sheet and bake for about 6-10 minutes, but be very careful since coconut loves to burn. Remove from heat and let cool, then add to the rice mixture.

Currant, Cilantro & Almond Couscous
Yields 8 portions

Ingredients:
8 oz cous cous (by weight)
6 oz orange juice
6 oz chicken stock
1 Tbsp extra virgin olive oil

1 bunch cilantro (shaved from the stems)
$\frac{1}{2}$ cup of dried currants
$\frac{1}{2}$ cup toasted or blanched almonds, chopped
1 roasted red bell pepper, small dice
$\frac{1}{4}$ Tbsp kosher salt
$\frac{1}{4}$ Tbsp black pepper

Method:
Heat the liquids in a stock pot with the oil on the stove top and bring to a rolling boil. Turn off the heat, add the couscous and cover with a lid for 5 minutes. Remove the lid and fluff the couscous with a fork. Add the peppers, currants, almonds & seasoning, then mix thoroughly. This dish can be served warm or as a cool refreshing side as well. It goes great with my Apple Mango Chicken or the Stuffed Pork Tenderloin.

Parsnip & Roasted Garlic Puree
Yields about 6 portions

Ingredients:
1 ½ lbs parsnips, peeled and sliced (think carrot here, it's a root vegetable) and 3 Tbsp of kosher salt for the water
½ cup heavy cream
1½ Tbsp unsalted butter
½ tsp kosher salt
½ tsp black pepper
¼ cup roasted garlic

Method:
Put peeled, sliced parsnips into a deep pot with water and add about 3 Tbsp of kosher salt. Cook until tender over medium heat while simmering for about 30-45 minutes. Test for doneness using your paring knife (like you would for mashed potatoes or the roasted beets, your knife should fall straight through if cooked properly).

Drain the parsnips and place into a food processor. Add the remaining ingredients and blend until smooth and creamy, adjust salt and pepper as needed and serve. These work great underneath the Coca Cola Braised Beef Short Ribs or other fall or winter dishes.

Triple Olive Tapenade
Yields one cup of tapenade

Ingredients:
¼ cup California black olives
¼ cup Kalamata black olives
¼ cup green Spanish olives
2 Tbsp sun dried tomatoes (dry, not in oil -but you can use those if you like)
2 Tbsp roasted garlic
¼ Tbsp black pepper

Method:
Blend everything in a food processor or blender until somewhat smooth. Make sure everything is mixed together, colors are blended and taste for seasoning. There is no salt added since the olives have the briny flavor with them already. This tapenade is so versatile it can be used with your bread at dinner, as a spread on a sandwich or to top off your favorite grilled fish.

Sweet & Sour Pickles

Yields a quart of pickles that store well in the fridge for late night snacking.

Ingredients:
1 ½ qts of sliced cucumbers from the mandolin (paper thin)
1/8 Tbsp nutmeg
1 ½ cups sugar
1 tsp black pepper
1 cup cider vinegar
¾ Tbsp kosher salt
1 tsp mustard seeds
¾ Tbsp celery seeds
1 cup white vinegar
¼ Tbsp turmeric

Method:
Mix all of the ingredients together except for cucumbers in a deep stock pot and place on the stovetop. Adjust to high heat, add the sliced cucumbers and bring to a full boil. Once boil is achieved, turn off the heat and set aside. Let the pickles cool and then you can store them in the pickling liquid in the fridge for a good 2-3 weeks. These work great on both my Ground Chicken and Tasty Turkey Burgers.

House Made Guac'
Yields just about 3-4 cups of guac

Ingredients:
4 medium, ripe Haas avocados (save pit to help prevent browning)
1Tbsp fresh lime juice
¼ tsp Chipotle Tabasco
1 tsp cumin powder
½ Tbsp kosher salt
1 tsp black pepper
1 tsp sugar

Method:
Remove avocados from skin by slicing in half, removing the pit and using a spoon to remove the good stuff. Set aside one or two pits that you can add to the guac to prevent browning. Mix all ingredients in a non-reactive bowl with a whisk or fork and make sure everything is well blended. Double check for seasonings, especially the salt since every avocado is different. Store covered with plastic wrap touching the guac and place in fridge until you are ready to serve. This is a great side to go with the Citrus Marinated Flank Steak or your favorite tortilla chips.

**side note-I know I do not have tomatoes & onions and such in my guac but for me it's really all about the avocado. What can I say, I'm a purist! If I want salsa with my avocado, I'll ask for it. Also the key here really is the Haas avocado for the creamy texture and flavor. If you can't get them in your area, adjust the seasonings accordingly to make it the best you can.

Apple Wood Bacon Refried Black Beans
Yields 4 cups or about 8 servings

Ingredients:
2 lbs black beans, canned with liquid
1 cup water
3 Tbsp apple wood bacon fat (rendered from cooked bacon)
¾ cup sweet onions, small dice
1 ½ Tbsp cumin powder
Kosher salt
Black pepper

Method:
Blend black beans and water in food processor or blender while heating bacon fat over medium high heat. Add chopped sweet onions into the heated fat and cook until caramelized; then add the cumin powder. Slowly pour the blended bean mixture into the cooked onions and cumin and cook over low heat until all of the fat integrates into the beans and the mixture begins to thicken. Add salt and pepper to taste. Serve with my Citrus Marinated Flank Steak or on the side with your favorite Mexican meal or as a bean dip at a party. The bacon fat really adds some great flavor to a timeless classic.

Queso Fundido (melted cheese dip)
Yields about 4 cups of cheesy goodness

Ingredients:
¾ cup cotija anejo (fine grate) -like a romano cheese
¾ cup queso fresco (fine grate)-like a mild feta
¼ cup Spanish goat cheese (Caprichevre if you can find it or
other dry style goat cheese)
1 cup pepper jack cheese (fine grate)

½ cup chorizo Leon (cut into ¼ inch pieces and then small dice
or other lean chorizo) - spicy pork chorizo
¼ cup roasted red bell pepper (canned-chopped small dice)
¼ cup roasted hatch green chiles (stems and seeds removed,
small dice)
¼ cup fire roasted garlic
½ cup oven roasted mushrooms (pg. 23)
1 tsp black pepper

Corn or Flour Tortillas
Toasted Corn Chips

Method:
Blend all ingredients together thoroughly in a bowl. Bake off
in individual tapas pans, similar baking dish or cast iron skillet
in 350 degree oven for about 12-15 minutes or until the cheese
is cooked through and bubbly. This dish is best served warm
with flour/corn tortillas or your favorite corn chips.

**It is very important to use the correct blend of cheeses due
to their fat content. If you use other cheeses, more oil/fat
may be present in the dish. The same applies to the type of
chorizo/sausage that you use since the Leon is not very oily

Queso Fundido, continued:

and very lean. If you have issues with too much oil/fat then you can use a paper towel to absorb it before serving to your guests.

** Where to buy hatch chiles-you can purchase these at New Mexican Connection (http://www.newmexicanconnection.com)

The Specialty Spanish Cheeses and Sausages- You can get all of these online at La Espanola Meats (http://www.laespanolameats.com)

Munchables......

I love me some Munchables and I don't mean the nasty snacks on the market called 'Lunchables'. The way that I like to enjoy my meals or when I am dining out is by having little bites of many dishes and sharing, mixing and matching them together. This cavalcade of delights has something that everyone is bound to call a favorite.

Pan Roasted Mussels are really one of the simplest dishes to prepare and they don't break the bank either. You will want to use PEI mussels which are from the Prince Edward Islands off the coast of Canada. If you can't find these locally, then use the best and freshest mussels you can find. I wanted to show you a simple way to showcase these tasty little morsels and in this case, less is more. The way to go is with some white wine, seasonings and topping it off with some toasty, crusty bread or a baguette for the broth. Try my Smoked Paprika Aioli on your bread before you toast it for a real treat, and if you want to forego the bread, you can actually zip up your dish by serving a dollop of the Aioli on your mussels after they have been pan roasted and let it melt into the broth.

I talked earlier about making a feast or a fiesta out of some of my Mexican/Latin American recipes and the Citrus Marinated Flank Steak is a great opening act that can be featured in tacos or just to nibble on with before you get things started.

My Lamb Meatball recipe came about while I was still at 'Crave'. I was always trying to keep an eye on food costs and save money in the kitchen. So one day I noticed that we had quite a bit of scraps left from the cleaning/Frenching of our lamb racks and I decided to grind the scraps and put some seasonings, breadcrumbs and egg together to create a tasty little meatball that became a popular starter on the menu. Serve with your favorite marinara or my 'Better than Great'

Marinara from the first book and you have a real winning combination.

On our journey to Asia via Munchables, I wanted to share some fun snacks like my Shrimp & Veggie Dumplings and Vietnamese Spring Rolls with dipping sauces to share (Tangy Soy Sauce & Nuoc Cham). The Dumplings are pan fired in very little oil and the Spring Rolls are light & crispy, full with fresh veggies and served cool with no cooking at all. These two dishes can start off your own Asian Invasion any day of the week. Both can be made in advance and you can simply finish off the Dumplings at service with a quick pan fry. The Spring Rolls can just hang out in the fridge until you are ready to munch.

Alright, I hope that no one is getting worked up over my Goat Cheese & Green Apple Ravioli. I know that it may sound a little funky but the two flavors together with a fabulous meat sauce or Dave's Bolognese from the first book is a treat for the senses. The apple, goat cheese, meat sauce and tomato flavors all come together wonderfully; add a glass of Oregon Pinot Noir and you and your guests may actually come to tears at the table.

For those that love chicken fingers/tenders (but are afraid to admit it aside from all of the kids across the country), I have included my Free Range Chicken Tenders (for adults if you use the Chipotle Glaze or How-Now, Kung Pao Sauce and keep them plain for kids). The recipes for these typically dangerous bar room snacks are lighter for you since there is no deep frying involved. It's all about full flavor but using less fat when you can...Do you see a healthy trend here in my kitchen?

We are also using better quality chicken, thus resulting in a higher quality product for everyone to enjoy. You definitely can't go wrong with either of the finishing or dipping sauces and you could even do batches of both for larger gatherings.

I have always been a fan of smoked or cured salmon when it's done right and not covered in Dill -yuck. If you are a salmon fan like me, then I encourage you to give my Salt & Brown Sugar Cured Salmon a try. It's all about advanced planning with this dish since you need a couple of days in order for the fish to cure properly. The fish does all the work, you just need to spend a little time getting it ready. This is a great dish for Brunches with my Bloody Marys from the Cocktail section and can be served with the Crispy Potato Pancakes from the Salad of Duck Confit recipe section. It also works great with your own Eggs Benedict- instead of using Canadian bacon you can use your own cured salmon.

So spend a little time in the kitchen in advance and then sit back and enjoy plenty of fantastic flavors & fun times in the land of Dave's Munchables.

Pan Roasted Mussels
Yields about 2 servings

Ingredients:
30 each PEI mussels (Prince Edward Island- a Canadian province where the mussels are farmed- and the ones I prefer to use for this dish)
½ cup bottled white wine (not box)
4-5 cloves roasted garlic
1 Tbsp shallots, chopped
1 Tbsp butter, unsalted

1 Tbsp basil, chiffonade
1 Tbsp tomato, chopped
Pinch of crushed red pepper flakes
Pinch of kosher salt and pepper

Toasted bread or baguette
Smoked Paprika Aioli (pg.53)

Method:
Heat a skillet to high heat. Add the butter, white wine and shallots and get everything heated through, allowing the wine to reduce just a bit. Drop in the roasted garlic and cleaned mussels and cook until the shells begin to open. (If you have any mussels with pre-opened shells- discard them and check the others for freshness. It's very important to know where your fish comes from and that it's quality). The process goes pretty quickly, so stand by your skillet and give the mussels a good shake about the pan so that they all get some of the heat and liquid to cook them. Once the shells begin to open, drop in your tomato, basil, crushed red pepper, salt and pepper so that everything gets well seasoned. Serve with toasted bread for dipping in the sauce.

Pan Roasted Mussels, continued:

You can also find the method for toasting the bread with my smoked paprika aioli, which is a perfect match to go with these simple and tasty pan roasted mussels.

Smoked Paprika Aioli (for the bread for the mussels)
Yields one cup of aioli

Ingredients:
1 Tbsp roasted garlic
2 egg yolks
1 tsp Dijon mustard

1 cup corn oil
$\frac{1}{4}$ tsp black pepper
$\frac{3}{4}$ tsp salt
$\frac{1}{4}$ tsp sugar
$\frac{1}{2}$ tsp lemon juice
$\frac{1}{2}$ tsp smoked paprika
$\frac{1}{2}$ tsp orange zest

Method:
In a mixer/blender add garlic, yolks and Dijon mustard and blend until the mixture turns more white than yellow. Slowly drizzle in the corn oil then add seasonings and lemon juice. Mix in a separate bowl if needed to make sure all ingredients are brought together and then store in the fridge at all times to avoid spoilage. Great in the summer with lobster rolls or as a sandwich spread.

Smoked Paprika Aioli, continued:

Bread for the mussels:

Slice open your baguette or brioche roll and spread the aioli onto both sides and place under your broiler for toasty goodness.

The aioli works like butter to give you the browning effect but has lots more flavor. Once toasty, remove from the broiler and serve with the Pan Roasted Mussels.

Citrus Marinated Flank Steak
Yields 2 ½ lbs of flank steak/enough for 6 dinner portions

Ingredients:
2 ½ -3 lbs of flank steak
½ cup fresh orange juice
¼ cup fresh lemon juice
¼ Tbsp garlic powder
¼ Tbsp onion powder
¼ cup corn oil
½ Tbsp salt
 Pinch of black pepper
¼ Tbsp sugar
¼ tsp cumin
1 Tbsp honey

Kosher salt
Black pepper

House Made Guac (pg.44)
Apple wood Bacon Refried Black Beans (pg.45)
Roasted Tomato Salsa (pg. 79)
One Dozen Flour or Corn Tortillas

Method:
Remove any fat from the flank steak and cut into small 3 inch strips. Blend all of the marinade ingredients in a blender/food processor or with a whisk in a non-reactive bowl until completely blended. In a large pyrex dish, bowl or plastic zip bag, add the strips of flank steak along with the marinade. I only allow the meat to marinade for about 3 hours because all the citrus juices start to cook the meat instead of tenderize it if you go too much longer than a couple of hours. The majority of all of my other marinades I recommend

Citrus Marinated Flank Steak, continued:

overnight, but with this one the citrus is too much for the protein. Remove the meat from the marinade and season it with the 50/50 blend of salt and pepper. You can either pan sear the meat in a hot skillet with a little bit of oil or grill to your desired temperature. The strips cook really quickly so keep a watch on them so you don't overcook them. Serve the cooked meat with your warm tortilla shells and all the fixings for a Taco Fiesta.

Lamb Meatballs
Yields about (15) 3oz meatballs

Ingredients:
2 ½ lbs boneless leg of lamb or lamb scraps (run through meat grinder by your butcher or at home if you have a grinder)
1 Tbsp garlic powder
1 Tbsp onion powder
1 Tbsp ground nutmeg
1 Tbsp ground oregano
1 Tbsp ground cumin
3 Tbsp 50/50 kosher salt and pepper blend
5 eggs
½ cup seasoned Italian breadcrumbs
½ cup Pecorino Romano cheese

Extra Virgin Olive Oil for browning, sautéing
Your favorite marinara or the one from my first book can be served as a sauce with the cooked meatballs

Method:
Blend all of the ingredients together in a large mixing bowl and make sure that the seasoning is mixed thoroughly. I usually use my hands but make sure that you wash them thoroughly or wear gloves. Once completely blended, form into 2 ½ - 3 oz meatballs and set aside until you cook them off.
Heat a large skillet or pan with olive oil then drop in the meatballs and cook slowly over low-medium heat until cooked through. Remove from the pan and serve with your favorite marinara, meat sauce and pasta noodle and you're good to go...Badda Bing.

Lamb Meatballs, continued:

**I love to serve these as an appetizer, just giving my guests 1-2 meatballs with some of my 'Better than Great' Marinara from Volume 1 and topping them off with some grated Parmesan and fresh basil

** You can also substitute ground sirloin for the lamb if you don't do the lamb thing.

Pan Fried Shrimp & Veggie Dumplings
Yields about 10 dumplings

Ingredients:
¼ cup shrimp, chopped, peeled and deveined
2 Tbsp carrots, julienne & chopped
¼ cup Shitake mushrooms, chopped, no stems
2 Tbsp water chestnuts, chopped
¼ cup Savoy/Napa cabbage, chopped
½ Tbsp egg (white and yolk mixed together)
2 Tbsp tangy soy sauce (pg. 61)

1 pkg round dumpling wrappers or gyoza skins (found in Asian markets and most grocery stores in the refrigerated section)
1 large egg
1 Tbsp water
Pinch of kosher salt
Pastry brush
Cornstarch
Canola oil for frying

Method:
Prepare and finely chop all veggies & shrimp. Blend with egg and tangy soy sauce and mix thoroughly in a small mixing bowl. Heat a skillet or wok with a small amount of canola oil and add the shrimp and veggies. Quickly cook over high heat. Veggies should still be crunchy but shrimp should be cooked or opaque in color. Next, drain any remaining liquid from the mixture in a colander and let the filling cool. In a separate bowl, mix the egg, water and kosher salt and set aside. Set up a clean counter space or cutting board in preparation for your dumpling assembly. I usually sprinkle a very small amount of cornstarch onto my work surface which helps the dumplings from sticking during assembly and storage.

Pan Fried Shrimp & Veggie Dumplings, continued:

You will want to work fast because the dumpling wrappers will dry out, so keep them covered and have your workstation all set up and ready to roll. Lay out a series of dumpling wrappers on your clean surface with the floured side up (each wrapper should have one side that appears to have more flour on it which aids in the sealing process, but if you cannot see a difference then just place either side down). Fill each wrapper with about one full Tablespoon of filling placed in the center of the wrapper. Using your pastry brush, dip into the egg and water mixture and paint the entire rim of the wrapper, folding the sides into each other and seal tightly by working the edges with your finger tips. Do not use too much liquid to seal the wrappers, you just need a little bit and can use your clean finger if you don't have a pastry brush lying around. Be sure that your wrapper does not bust or have any holes in it, if it does than discard and start over using less filling. Set up a sheet tray or baking pan where you will store the prepared dumplings after assembly. I also place a little cornstarch on the bottom of the tray/pan to keep dumplings sticking together and layer each row with waxed paper or plastic wrap to keep them from touching one another or lightly dust with cornstarch (but remove it before pan frying).

Heat a small amount of canola oil in a skillet or wok, and by small I mean 1-2 Tbsp of oil just to get a shine on the pan/wok. Once pan is heated, cook a couple of dumplings at a time over medium high heat. Your goal here is to get some color onto the wrapper and reheat the ingredients on the inside. Again, you want to work fast here and serve the dumplings immediately. If you are doing several dumplings and they are all pan fried, you can set them all back into the pan, put in a small amount of water and cover with a lid over low heat to keep them warm

Pan Fried Shrimp & Veggie Dumplings, continued:

and heated through. Serve with more of the Tangy Soy Sauce, Dave's Peanut Sauce or my How, Now-Kung Pao Sauce

Tangy Soy Sauce
Yields almost ½ cup of sauce

Ingredients:
1 Tbsp mushroom soy sauce
2 Tbsp sweet soy sauce
1 Tbsp LITE soy sauce
½ Tbsp red chili/garlic sauce
1 Tbsp seasoned rice vinegar
½ Tbsp fish sauce

Method:
In small mixing bowl add all ingredients and whisk together. Use to season the dumpling mixture and serve as a dipping sauce.

Vietnamese Style Veggie Spring Rolls
Yields about 4-6 spring rolls

Ingredients:
2Tbsp straw mushrooms (chopped)
2Tbsp baby corn (chopped)
6Tbsp carrots, julienned
1 cup mixed blend of purple and green cabbage (julienned)
1 $\frac{1}{2}$ Tbsp oyster sauce
$\frac{1}{4}$ cup of bean sprouts
$\frac{1}{4}$ cup cucumber, julienned
1 Tbsp Thai basil, chopped (regular basil if you can't find the Thai variety)
1 Tbsp mint, chopped
1 Tbsp cilantro, chopped
$\frac{1}{2}$ tsp 50/50 –kosher salt and black pepper mix

8 each, 8 $\frac{1}{2}$ inch Dried Rice Wrappers/Papers (Asian markets)

Method:
Blend all veggies, herbs and seasoning in a medium sized bowl and set aside.
Fill a large bowl half full of hot water (but not scalding, as you will have to dip your fingers in it). Place bowl and wrappers on a clean working station, such as a cutting board. Take out one of the rice wrappers and place it in the bowl of hot water. You may have to gently press the wrapper down into the water. The rice paper will soften in about 30 seconds. When the wrapper is soft enough to eat (as they do not require any cooking), remove from the water and place on your clean workstation.
Working always horizontally, place your veggie/herb mixture toward the end of the wrapper. Begin to roll by folding the bottom portion of rice paper over the ingredients.

62

Vietnamese Style Spring Rolls, continued:

Continue by lifting the right side of the wrapper and folding it over the ingredients. To complete the roll, fold top side down, OR roll the spring roll forward until the end of the rice paper. Try to keep your folding/rolling as tight as possible. The ingredients should appear at one end to create an "open" type of fresh roll. To secure the roll, simply dip your fingers in a little water and wet the end flap, then press to seal. Place upright in a bowl (like a bouquet), or on a platter. Serve with the Nuoc Cham or Dave's Peanut Sauce and get ready for an explosion of freshness.

Dipping Sauce for Spring Rolls (Nuoc Cham)
Yields about 1 cup of sauce

Ingredients:
$\frac{1}{4}$ Tbsp ground dried red chiles (chopped and diced)
1 $\frac{1}{4}$ Tbsp lime juice
$\frac{1}{4}$ cup rice wine vinegar
6 Tbsp of Mirin (Asian markets)
$\frac{1}{2}$ cup simple syrup (made with $\frac{1}{4}$ cup water & $\frac{1}{4}$ cup sugar cooked to a high boil)

Method:
Make simple syrup by blending water and sugar in a sauce pan and cooking to a high boil. Add the remaining ingredients to the simple syrup. Let cool before use as the dipping sauce. If you like it really hot, you can add heat by adding more red chiles to the sauce. Serve with the Vietnamese Style Veggie Rolls.

Goat Cheese & Green Apple Ravioli
Yields about 30 ravioli

Ingredients:
1 Granny Smith Apple (cored, sliced with skin on)
11 oz goat cheese
$\frac{1}{2}$ tsp nutmeg
$\frac{1}{2}$ tsp cinnamon
$\frac{1}{4}$ Tbsp black pepper
$\frac{1}{4}$ Tbsp granulated sugar
$\frac{1}{4}$ tsp kosher salt

Fresh pasta sheets (actually on amazon.com if you can't find them at your grocery or in the frozen section)
Gyoza wrappers/skins (alternative if you can't find the pasta sheets available at Asian markets or your grocery)
Flour for the pastry sheets OR Cornstarch for the gyoza skins
2 $\frac{1}{2}$ inch Ring cutter/biscuit cutter (you can find whole sets of these on cookiecutter.com)
1 large egg
Pinch of Kosher salt
Pastry brush

Your favorite meat sauce or Dave's Bolognese & Sherry Cream Sauce from FQ, Vol. 1

Method:
Place the apples and goat cheese in food processor, add seasonings and blend. I like to put the mixture in the fridge for a bit to cool before trying to assemble the ravioli. The method for these is very similar to the Pan Fried Dumplings if you are using the gyoza skins. Whisk together your egg and salt in a small mixing bowl. If you are using the pasta sheets, you will need the ring/biscuit cutter or you could use a

Goat Cheese & Green Apple Ravioli, continued:

sharp paring knife around a glass with the same diameter- but the cutter is more accurate. Set up a clean workstation and lay out a little bit of flour and your pasta sheet. Take a heaping Tablespoon of your cooled filling, set rows of them onto the sheet and then use your cutter to cut out the base/filling portion of your ravioli. Next, come through and cut the same size (but add no filling) with your cutter for the top portion of the ravioli. Remove the base portion and paint around the border of it with your egg/salt mixture, then place the top of your ravioli and tightly pinch together and seal the edges.

You will want to store these in a baking dish or sheet tray with some flour in between each ravioli along with wax/plastic wrap so that they do not get stuck together. Make sure they do not touch each other and stay separate to avoid complications later. Your ravioli is ready to cook or store for later service.

If you are using the gyoza skins/wrappers, then you will use the cornstarch method and they may hold closer to a Tablespoon but not a heaping one and follow the same directions for preparation and storage as the Pan Fried Dumplings. You will cook both versions of the ravioli in the same method below.

Heat a stock pot with water and kosher salt and bring to a rolling boil. Drop in a few of either ravioli at a time but do not overcrowd the pot or the temperature will drop and your ravioli will not cook. The gyoza cook pretty quickly and the regular pasta will take a few minutes for the dough to cook and heat the filling. You can always check one for doneness until you get the hang of it. Once they are all cooked, you can serve them on a base of your favorite meat sauce and top with grated Parmesan.

Goat Cheese & Green Apple Ravioli, continued:

My preferred method involves two recipes from my first book, the Sherry Cream Sauce from 'Out of the Bleu' along with Dave's Bolognese. I place a small amount of the Sherry Cream on the base of the plate and top with my ravioli, finishing with a couple healthy spoonfuls of the Bolognese and garnish with Parmesan. The combo is fantastic together and worth the time and effort.

Free Range Chicken Tenders
Yields enough tenders for 3-4 guests

Ingredients:
1 lb Free Range chicken breast or tenders (cut into strips)
1 ¾ cups Japanese rice flour (Mochi) - found at Asian markets
2 ½ Tbsp kosher salt
1 Tbsp black pepper

2 large eggs
Pinch of kosher salt
Canola Oil

Method:
In a medium mixing bowl add all of the dry ingredients and set aside. Whisk together the 2 eggs/salt and place in a small bowl. Clean your chicken and then set up a plate with the dry mixture next to the bowl with the blended eggs. Dip your chicken into the egg and then roll and cover completely in the flour mixture. The Japanese rice flour is so light and delicate it really makes a difference in the final product. Once all of your tenders have gone through the egg and flour mixture, place a small amount of canola oil (1-2 Tbsp) into a skillet over high heat and cook your tenders for about 2 minutes each side or until cooked through. When they are just finishing cooking, turn off the heat and add a couple of Tablespoons of either the Chipotle Glaze or Kung Pao Sauce into the skillet/pan. Let it heat up with the chicken, coating all of the tenders, and you can add a little heat if you need to get the sauce all warmed up. You can serve them plain with the sauces on the side, but I love to use the method above for tastier tenders. If you do use the chipotle glaze, you can serve them up with my Cool Gorgonzola Sauce from my first book for the perfect finish.

Free Range Chicken Tenders, continued:

**These are a nice option for kids and you can keep them plain without the sauces. Since there is no deep frying it's a much better choice than the frozen chicken nuggets on the market.

Chipotle Glaze
Yields about 1 ½ cups of glaze

Ingredients:
¼ cup Chipotle Tabasco
¼ cup regular Tabasco
¼ lb unsalted butter
¾ cups granulated sugar
½ tsp kosher salt

Method:
In a small saucepan, add all the ingredients and heat on high until butter is melted and you are good to go. Set aside and serve with the Free Range Chicken Tenders.

How, Now- Kung Pao Sauce
Yields about 1 ½ cups of sauce

Ingredients:
2 oz brown sugar
½ cup red chili garlic sauce
¼ cup sweet soy sauce
½ Tbsp fish sauce
¼ cup dark mushroom soy sauce
¼ cup rice wine vinegar
¼ cup honey

How, Now-Kung Pao Sauce, continued:

Method:
Blend all of the ingredients together in a medium size bowl with a whisk. If using this as a dipping sauce, you will need to heat all of the ingredients in a small sauce pan on the stovetop over medium heat for about 3-5 minutes in order to get everything working together and reduced a bit. This sauce can be used for your own version of Spicy Asian Wings or as a marinade (uncooked). You can oven bake the wings versus deep frying for a healthier alternative to deep fried chicken wings. Or use this glaze to finish off your tenders in the pan.

Salt & Brown Sugar Cured Salmon

Yields about 2-3 lbs cured salmon

** This is a 3 day process, so plan ahead if you want to do this recipe. It's not difficult; you just need the time for the curing process.

Dry Rub
Ingredients:

4 oz fresh lime juice (to coat the fish before applying the dry rub)

4 oz salt

4 oz brown sugar

1 ¼ Tbsp black pepper

Wet Rub
Ingredients:

4 oz molasses

1 ¼ Tbsp smoked paprika

1 ¼ Tbsp black pepper

2-3 lbs fresh Salmon, cleaned of pin bones, skin off
Pastry brush

Method:
Day One-

Clean salmon and place on perforated hotel pan inside another hotel pan or at home set inside a pyrex dish. Paint the fish in lime juice, then apply and coat all of the fish in the dry rub, really covering up all exposed parts of the fish on the surface. Next, place another hotel pan or smaller, narrower dish or pan on top of the fish to weigh it down and place in the refrigerator covered with plastic wrap for at least 2 days to cure.

Salt & Brown Sugar Cured Salmon, continued:

Make sure that the pans/trays you use can hold liquid because the fish will leech out liquids during the curing process.

Day Three-
Remove the salmon from the fridge and wash off the dry cure/rub from the salmon. Don't get crazy here with the rinsing just a gentle rinse under cool water to remove the salt cure. Gently pat dry and set the salmon onto a sheet tray or platter. Heat the wet rub ingredients and let cool for a little bit. Using your pastry brush, paint the wet rub onto the salmon. Now place the salmon back into the fridge for 12 hours uncovered so that it can from a pellicle (a thin film or membrane that covers the fish). After the final 12 hour period, your salmon is cured and ready to serve with brunch or with your favorite bagel and cream cheese.

The Big Dippers...

In my house/kitchen, it's always been 'all about the sauce'. I love sauces, dips, rubs and marinades so much because they really enhance the meal and give you more flavors to savor. In this sampling of some of my favorite sauces, I'm starting out with a sauce that took me a lot of work to nail down- Dave's Peanut Sauce. I really wanted to capture all of the wonderful nuances of SouthEast Asia in this delicate and delicious sauce. It uses an aromatic curry paste which is the key for me versus using powders; and you can order them online for your Asian cooking sessions at home. The lime, sweet chili, coconut milk and brown sugar along with the fish sauce make this a balanced sauce perfect for satay. You can even turn it into lite vinaigrette for a salad by adding some seasoned rice vinegar. Trust me, you and your friends will love this re-creation of a classic.

When putting together a pesto sauce, I really wanted to mellow out the flavor by using roasted garlic and walnut in lieu of the traditional pine nut and raw garlic. My Walnut & Basil Pesto also has significantly less oil than most so that the flavor of the basil, cheeses and nuts comes through resulting in a great spread for sandwiches, a great finish to your favorite pasta dish or a treat on top of your favorite eggs or omelets.

My Tangy Shallot, White Wine & Mustard Sauce is a savory and tangy blend of ingredients that come together to finish a pan roasted salmon, or can work with other fish and poultry dishes as well when you want something different.

In modifying the classic Greek sauce, Tzatziki, my principle of always utilizing roasted garlic instead of raw results in the same traditional flavors but with more balance and not so much bite that it overwhelms the rest of your gyro. I always feel that it's important that one specific flavor does not rule the dish and to allow all of the flavors to work in harmony so that you have a pleasant journey on your 'Flavor Quest'. Using Greek yogurt also makes a huge difference in flavor, but if you can't find it, simply strain your regular yogurt through cheesecloth to remove the liquids and you will end up with a thicker product and tastier Tzatziki in the end (thanks Brent B.).

What can I say about a great salsa except, 'I love you'. For me it's always about the roasted and blended varieties since they allow for more flavor and keep the ingredients from competing with each other (like in a pico de gallo or other chopped salsas). I'm not saying those are bad but I'm not a fan of raw onion so that's why the majority of my salsas are blended and typically have oven roasted ingredients in them. Food is very personal and subjective and that's why we all have such strong opinions when it comes to food. The mix of the sweet onion, fire roasted tomatoes & roasted garlic results in a mellow salsa with a tad of heat from the chipotle/adobo.

The easy Spicy Sweet Honey Mustard is nothing more than a quick blend of ingredients that you typically have at home which turns your Dijon into something more than just what it is by using fresh citrus and honey to balance it out and give it some zing. You can keep it on hand as a new condiment or dipping sauce for when you want something more than just a plain mustard or Dijon.

My Sweet Onion & Apple Compote comes together pretty quickly and can be served with cured meats, pork and as a side to a cheese plate. It has a nice balance of sweet and savory with the warmth of nutmeg and cinnamon that really work well with the apples, sweet onions and dried currants. It's a super versatile little dish that people enjoy , so see what you can pair it with and let me know what you like serving it with at your house.

Dave's Peanut Sauce
Yields 1 cup of sauce

Ingredients:
Splash of peanut or canola oil
½ shallot, finely chopped
2 cloves roasted garlic, diced
½ Tbsp Curry paste (yellow, green or red-yellow is the most mild, green and red have more heat-available at Asian markets or amazon.com, my favorite brand is Mae Ploy)

5 oz coconut milk
4 oz smooth peanut butter, old fashioned style works best if you can get it
½ Tbsp. fish sauce
¼ cup sweet chili sauce (Mae Ploy brand here again)
¼ cup brown sugar
½ lime, fresh squeezed for the juice
6 oz chicken stock

Method:
In a saucepan, heat up oil, shallot, garlic and curry paste until it becomes aromatic/fragrant over medium heat. Next, add all of the other ingredients and whisk together and heat through for about 5-10 minutes. Remove from heat and cool. You can also use an immersion blender or table top blender to achieve a smoother consistency for your sauce. It's totally up to you and for me it depends on my mood, sometimes I do and sometimes I don't. This sauce is perfect with my Pork Satay. You can also use with the Veggie Dumplings and Spring Rolls.

Walnut & Basil Pesto
Yields 1 cup of pesto

Ingredients:
½ cup Toasted walnuts
2 Tbsp roasted garlic
2 cups basil (firmly packed in cup)
½ cup Parmesan cheese
½ cup Romano cheese
1 tsp black pepper
1 tsp kosher salt
½ cup extra virgin olive oil

Method:
Blend all ingredients in a food processor/blender until completely blended, but do not overwork it as the basil will brown even more. Remove from the processor and be sure to put a little bit of olive oil on the top of the pesto for storage along with plastic wrap touching the pesto to prevent oxidation and discoloration. This pesto works great on your favorite sandwich like a BLT, fresh pasta or as a simple party dip with toasted baguettes.

Tangy Shallot, White Wine & Mustard Sauce
Yields about 1 ½ cups of sauce

Ingredients:
2 Tbsp extra virgin olive oil
1 Tbsp unsalted butter

¾ cups shallots, small dice
6 oz sherry wine
¾ cup Sauvignon Blanc wine
2 Tbsp Dijon mustard
1 ½ cups veggie stock
6 cloves roasted garlic (smashed)
2 Tbsp cold butter
Pinch of cinnamon and nutmeg
1 tsp honey
¼ Tbsp black pepper

Method:
Heat oil and butter in a medium size sauté pan then add your
shallots. Cook until nicely caramelized and they have some
color on them. Next, deglaze with the sherry and add the
white wine, cooking until it is dry again. Add the remaining
ingredients and cook on stove top over medium heat for about
7-10 minutes or until it has started to reduce and have some
thickness/body. Adjust seasoning with kosher salt and pepper
as needed. This sauce works nicely over a simple pan roasted
piece of salmon. I am also recommending it with the Stuffed
Pork Tenderloin.

Tzatziki Sauce
Yields about 2 cups of Tzatziki

Ingredients:
1 cup plain yogurt (goat or cow's milk)
1 fresh lemon, juiced
4 Tbsp roasted garlic, chopped
1 seedless English cucumber (peeled, halved, and diced small)
1 Tbsp mint leaves, finely chopped
Kosher salt and freshly ground black pepper, to taste

Method:
Place cucumbers in a sieve or colander for 15-20 minutes and allow the water to drain out of them. Once cucumbers are drained, place all of the ingredients into a mixing bowl and combine with a fork. Refrigerate for at least 1 hour to allow the flavors to marry together. Serve this with some roasted lamb, beef skewers or as a cool refreshing dip for your veggies.

Roasted Tomato Salsa
Yields 2 cups of salsa

Ingredients:
8 oz canned fire roasted tomatoes plus liquid
8 oz chopped and caramelized sweet onions (cooked until heavily caramelized in EVO)
1 Tbsp chipotle and adobo
1 Tbsp red wine vinegar
8 cloves roasted garlic
½ Tbsp fresh lemon juice
1 ½ tsp kosher salt
½ tsp black pepper
1 tsp granulated sugar

Method:
Heat a medium sized sauté pan over high heat, add some EVO, then add the chopped sweet onions and cook for about 10 minutes or until lots of color/caramelization is achieved. Blend all of the ingredients in the food processor, but you can leave some small chunks if you like. You will really need to double check for salt, pepper and sugar after the salsa is blended. After the salsa has been cooled, the flavors can change, so when you remove from the fridge take another taste before your guests start munching on it. This is a super match for the Citrus Marinated Flank Steak or serve alongside my House Made Guac' with your favorite tortilla chips.

Spicy Sweet Honey Mustard
Yields 1 cup of honey mustard

Ingredients:
$\frac{3}{4}$ cups Dijon mustard
$\frac{1}{2}$ cup honey
$\frac{1}{2}$ tsp kosher salt
$\frac{1}{2}$ tsp black pepper
4 Tbsp fresh orange juice
$\frac{1}{4}$ Tbsp fresh lemon juice

Method:
In a medium sized mixing bowl, blend all ingredients together with a whisk and then store in the refrigerator. This dip works with the Free Range Chicken Tenders or on my Ground Chicken and Tasty Turkey Burgers, as well.

Sweet Onion & Apple Compote
Yields about 1 cup of compote

Ingredients:
½ Tbsp extra virgin olive oil
½ Tbsp unsalted butter
1 Granny Smith apple (Cored, not peeled, small dice)
¼ cup sweet onion, small dice
¼ cup of dried currants or raisins
1 Tbsp of granulated sugar
¼ tsp cinnamon
¼ tsp nutmeg
½ tsp kosher salt
¼ tsp black pepper

Method:
On stovetop, heat up butter and oil in a medium sauté pan.
Add small dice of onions and caramelize these over medium
heat for about 5-7 minutes. Add the apples and the remaining
ingredients and cook them together for another 5 minutes or
until the apples have released some of their liquid but still
retain some of their texture. Set aside and serve with the
Crispy Potato Pancakes, my Hoisin & Cider Lamb or the
Stuffed Pork Tenderloin.

Entrees, Burger & More, Oh My...

There are some great dishes in this section that can work as the focal point of your meal or function fantastically on their own. If you have never used soda as a braising liquid, you are going to love what it does to tenderize meat, and if you have never braised before than you are probably going to love learning the method to slow cooked meats. Typically, most chefs use bone-in short ribs which you are welcome to do, especially if you can't find the boneless variety. Remember to adjust the quantity accordingly since there will be less yield due to the bones. My Smokey Rub really gives the short ribs a kick-start, followed by their extended bath in the Coca-Cola over the veggies, which can also be eaten with the dish. I like serving this with the Watermelon Salad and roasted corn on the cob for a lighter version of BBQ during the summer. In the winter, try this dish with the veggies and serve it with my Parsnip Puree for the perfect home cooked, hearty meal.

The Maple & Thyme Roasted Boneless Turkey Roast is perfect for the holidays for a small family or single person that wants the creature comforts of the holidays with a lot less effort. But just because it's turkey doesn't mean that it's just for the holidays! I created this recipe for a restaurant in NYC and we used the turkey for a turkey breast sandwich that was on the menu and then turned the roasted veggies from it to make our Turkey Pan Gravy for another dish. You'll notice that I don't normally use any thickening agents (like cornstarch, flour, arrowroot) in my sauces and soups since I'm not a fan of them and I believe in taking the extra time to slowly reduce and build up all of the flavors. The turkey can be used in a variety of ways and is deliciously moist and tender when you cook it properly. So feel free to enjoy this bird all year long.

My Apple Mango Chicken and Peach & Plum Salsa are a fantastic pair together or they can hang out separately. I use nut oil along with the apple and mango juices to add some more flavor to the chicken during the marinade process which helps to keep the chicken even more tender and from sticking to the pan or grill when you cook it off.

The marinade for my Hoisin & Cider Lamb Chops doubles as a marinade for my Pork Tenderloin Satay. You can use the Mango & Apricot Chutney on the lamb, as a savory spread for a yummy duck sandwich or warm it up and put it on top of a round of brie or other creamy cheese for a fun snack. The fresh apple cider is a key ingredient just like fresh juices in all of my recipes, but if you have an issue finding it then just grab the best quality apple juice/cider that you can find.

I have made the Wild Striped Bass for several events and people really love the idea of not really having a starch, but instead enjoying all of the Roasted Veggies and of course the Roasted Garlic Butter that finishes the dish. You can actually watch a video of me making the dish on www.behindtheburner.com. This dish has so many wonderful flavors and textures that it's sure to be a hit for a date night or larger gathering.

If you've never thought of trying a Stuffed Pork Tenderloin, well now's your chance. It's a fairly simple technique that adds so much more to a regular pork tenderloin. In this recipe, the mixture of goat cheese, figs, cinnamon & black pepper work nicely with the pork. You can try serving it with the Sweet Onion & Apple Compote or Tangy Shallot, White Wine & Mustard Sauce to give it that little something extra.

Both my Ground Chicken and Tasty Turkey Burgers stack up nicely on your favorite bun along with my Sweet & Sour Pickles. What makes these Burgers special is the right blend of special herbs and spices (we aren't talking about nasty Colonel Sanders special blend here). The Chicken Burger has ground oregano, Tabasco and fresh thyme that give the chicken a bold & zesty taste -

(definitely use the ground oregano since it has more flavor then the dry flake oregano). If you've never had ground chicken, realize that the texture is unique since there is not an over abundance of fat. Most people love it but I've had some guests that don't love the texture-- but I hope you will give it a chance. The Turkey Burger has a pinch of Worcestershire sauce that balances nicely with the fresh sage and cumin. You can't go wrong with either Burger especially if you are looking to have a lighter alternative to high fat ground beef burgers. My secret to both burgers is finishing them with a splash of white wine which adds a touch of flavor and moisture at the end of the cooking process.

Coca Cola Braised Boneless Beef Short Ribs

Yields about 3 lbs of short ribs or enough for about 8 guests as an entree

** This dish is two steps: seasoning/searing and the actual braising of the beef ribs.

Ingredients:

5 lbs of boneless beef short ribs, silver skin removed (you can use bone in ribs if you like or that's all that your market carries, I just prefer using the boneless)

1 cup Smokey Rub to season the ribs before braising (see below)

Veggies...

1 each sweet onion, large dice

1-2 each carrot, large dice

$\frac{1}{4}$ bunch of celery, large dice

4 oz cremini mushrooms, sliced

1 $\frac{1}{2}$ Tbsp 50/50 salt and pepper to cover veggies

64 oz Coca Cola (or enough to cover the meat for braising)

Extra Virgin Olive Oil

Foil

Method:

Slice all of the veggies and put into deep roasting pan/pyrex dish. Sprinkle them with kosher salt and black pepper and set aside. Next, slice pieces of short ribs into 1-2 inch slabs and roll them in my Smokey Rub. Heat a skillet or cast iron pan with some olive oil and sear off the pieces of seasoned short rib on all sides to lock in the flavor and seasonings. Do not overcrowd the pan while you are searing. (Note: You may need to wipe the pan down a couple of times due to the sugars in the rub.) Once you have finished searing all of the short ribs, lay

Coca Cola Braised Beef Short Ribs, continued:

them on top of the sliced veggies in your roasting pan and cover with the Coca Cola. Wrap the pan in foil and place into a pre-heated oven at 350 degrees for about 2 ½ -3 hours. Check for doneness at 2 ½ hours by seeing if the meat is ultra tender (kind of falling apart/melting in your mouth) and if so, then it's ready to be removed from the oven. Be careful of the hot steam trapped under the foil when checking for doneness. If it is not ready, cover and try another 30 minutes, then remove the roasting pan from the oven. Leave the foil on for the meat to continue to braise with the liquids and the steam (this will tenderize the short ribs even more). You can serve along with the veggies from the pan over my Parsnip Puree or mashed potatoes. These short ribs also go great with the Cider Vinegar BBQ Glaze from my first book as a BBQ dish served up with my Watermelon Salad.
**braise-a method of cooking where meat or veggies are cooked in oil/fat (seared) and then slow cooked using low heat resulting in a more tender and delicious product.

Smokey Rub (for Coca Cola Braised Beef Short Ribs)
Yields 5 cups of rub

Ingredients:
1 cup smoked paprika
1 cup kosher salt
1 ½ cups sugar
1 ½ cups brown sugar
2/3 cup cumin
2 Tbsp Ancho Chile powder, you can use regular Chile powder if you can't find ancho
½ cup black pepper
2 Tbsp ground oregano

Smokey Rub, continued:

Method:
Mix all ingredients together in a bowl and break up clumps of sugar or spices by hand. Use to rub onto the pieces of short ribs before searing and braising. Store in a cool, dry place for use on your other favorite meats or fish before cooking.

Maple & Thyme Roasted Boneless Turkey Roast
Yields enough for 8-12 guests

Ingredients:
1 each/3 lb defrosted Boneless Turkey Roast (remove string and split in half)
½ cup maple syrup
½ cup fresh thyme, add into the maple syrup above
50/50 blend of kosher salt and pepper to cover the bird

Veggies for the base:
¼ cup extra virgin olive oil
½ medium sized sweet onion, large dice
2 carrots, large dice
½ bunch celery, large dice
¼ cup fresh thyme

Method:
Take the defrosted bird, remove the string and unroll it. Place the olive oil and sliced veggies/thyme into your roasting pan. Completely season all of the turkey using the 50/50 salt and pepper blend and then place the bird in the pan on top of the seasoned veggies. Drizzle it with the maple syrup and thyme mixture and cover the pan in foil. Roast at 350 degrees for about 1½ -2 hours. Check the temperature at the 1½ hour mark, but be careful when lifting the foil because the trapped steam can be very hot and give you a nasty burn. If the bird is already at about 155 degrees, remove from the oven and let it rest with foil on it to reach the final temp of 165 degrees.

If you still need more time, pop it back in the oven to let it finish. Remove carefully from the oven and set on the stovetop to cool with foil on to retain moisture. If you are over 165 degrees, let it cool without the foil and place plastic wrap over the bird to lock in moisture. Do not throw out your veggies

Maple & Thyme Turkey Roast, continued:

and liquid, as they will be used for the Turkey Pan Gravy. This is a great holiday option if you don't have a large family or don't feel like cooking a whole bird. You can also serve it up with all the fixings for a holiday meal any time of year. It also works great for a hot or cold turkey sandwich, especially with the Turkey Pan Gravy.

Turkey Pan Gravy
Yields about 2 cups of tasty gravy

Ingredients:
2 cups veggies and pan drippings from Turkey Roast
$\frac{1}{2}$ cup heavy cream

Method:
Place the turkey drippings and veggies in a food processor or blender and blend completely. Transfer to a medium saucepan, add the cream and heat all ingredients together on the stove. This easy gravy is ready to roll. Serve along with the Turkey Roast.

Apple Mango Free Range Chicken
Serves 4- 6 guests

Ingredients:
4 cleaned Free Range, boneless chicken breasts (cut into 3-inch strips)
2 cups fresh apple cider (fresh is ideal or you can use another quality juice like Martinelli's)
2 cups mango juice or your favorite equivalent (i.e.: guava, pineapple or blend)
1 Tbsp black pepper
1 Tbsp kosher salt
2 Tbsp hazelnut oil (walnut or other nut oil will work, just steer away from sesame- I use La Tourangelle Oils)

Additional kosher salt and black pepper for seasoning after the marinating process

Method:
Remove any fat and cartilage from the chicken breast and cut into small 3 inch strips. In a medium sized bowl, whisk together juices, salt, pepper and nut oil. In a pyrex dish, container or Ziploc bag, lay the strips of chicken in the marinade and let them sit overnight for maximum results. You can marinade for as little as 2-3 hours if time is an issue. Remove the chicken from marinade and season both sides of the chicken with a pinch of kosher salt and black pepper (50/50 blend). Heat outdoor or indoor grill to high and place strips on, quickly grilling each side. Do not overcook the chicken as these little strips will cook in about 3-5 minutes total cooking time (remember some of the acids from the juices have broken down the chicken already). Remove cooked chicken from the grill and place in a new clean container. Cover with saran wrap or foil and let chicken rest

Apple Mango Free Range Chicken, continued:

(it will continue to cook, slightly). The chicken is really nice with my Toasted Coconut Rice and it can also be served warm or room temperature.

** This chicken is also awesome on top of my Grilled Summer Corn Salad from the first book and then finished with my Peach & Plum Salsa--it's such a great mix of flavors. I created this salad for my good friend Kristen Luken's shower back in Long Beach years ago and it's a real hit with everyone that's ever tried it since.

Peach & Plum Salsa (for Apple Mango Chicken)
Yields enough for 6-8 guests

Ingredients:
3 fresh plums (pit removed and cut into small pieces)
3 fresh peaches (pit removed and cut into small pieces)
2 Tbsp of your favorite honey
2 tsp ground cinnamon
$\frac{1}{4}$ tsp nutmeg
1 Tbsp fresh lemon juice
2 tsp black pepper

Method:
In a small bowl, place the sliced plums and peaches and add the remaining ingredients. Carefully mix using a fork or spatula, but mix gently to not break up all of the fruit.

This easy salsa works perfectly over my Apple Mango Chicken but could also work with the Stuffed Pork Tenderloin and with my Crème Fraiche Ice Cream.

Hoisin & Cider Lamb Chops & Pork Satay

Yields marinade for 2 lbs of Lamb Chops (Frenched) for about 6-8 guests or 2 lbs of Pork Tenderloin for 8-10 guests

** The pork satay is definitely a Munchable but I wanted to keep the recipe and method in this section since it made more sense.

Ingredients:

2 lbs Lamb Rib Chops, Frenched for Hoisin & Cider Lamb
OR
2 lbs Pork Tenderloin, cleaned and sliced in $\frac{1}{4}$ inch slices for Pork Satay

Marinade for Lamb or Pork

Ingredients:
10 oz Hoisin sauce
8 oz fresh apple cider
$\frac{1}{2}$ Tbsp black pepper

Extra Virgin Olive Oil
40-50 (4 $\frac{1}{2}$ inch) Bamboo skewers for Pork Satay

Lamb Rack Method:

Mix the marinated ingredients in a medium mixing bowl with a whisk. In a pyrex dish/Ziploc bag, pour the mixture over your cleaned lamb, making sure all of the lamb is covered completely and then store in the fridge. Let it marinade for at least 3-4 hours but ideally overnight. After you remove the lamb from the marinade, you can grill off the chops to your desired temperature or pan sear them in a medium sized skillet over medium to high heat with a little olive oil in the pan. I usually like to start the lamb with a sear in the pan and then put in a high heat oven at 450 degrees for about 3-5 minutes to finish

Hoisin & Cider Lamb Chops & Pork Satay, continued:

my lamb to medium rare. You can also start in the pan, turn down the heat, cover and finish on the stove top if you prefer. The lamb is really a great match for my Mango & Apricot Chutney. You can also pair with the Currant, Cilantro & Almond Couscous or the Parsnip Puree from the Side Kicks Chapter.

Pork Satay Method:
Take your thinly sliced pork tenderloin pieces and thread each piece onto one end of a bamboo skewer. Marinate them overnight in a baking dish, and then remove from the liquid before cooking. These can also be cooked on a grill if you have it, but be sure not to overcook your pork or it will be dry and not so good. The other method is to heat a skillet with a splash of olive oil over medium-high heat and then lay a couple of skewers down in the pan at a time to sear them off. They are so thin that you can cook them in the pan by turning off the heat and covering them with a lid to finish the cooking process, while keeping the moisture in the pork since it is so lean. You will want to serve these with my Peanut Sauce and you can see a visual of the dish on the back cover of on my website. For a complete entrée, this is a great dish that goes along with my Toasted Coconut Rice.

Mango & Apricot Chutney (for the Hoisin & Cider Lamb)
Yields about 3 cups of chutney

Ingredients:
1 oz unsalted butter
½ oz extra virgin olive oil
½ cup Sweet Onions (small dice)

Mango & Apricot Chutney, continued:

16 oz Major Grey's Mango Chutney
$\frac{1}{2}$ tsp Ground Cinnamon
1 Tbsp Brown Sugar
$\frac{1}{2}$ cup dried currants
1 Tbsp cilantro, chopped
1 Tbsp mint, chopped
$\frac{1}{2}$ cup dried apricots (chopped small dice)
$\frac{1}{4}$ Tbsp kosher salt
$\frac{1}{4}$ Tbsp black pepper

Method:
In a sauté/sauce pan, heat the butter and olive oil. Add the onions and caramelize heavily for about 5-7 minutes. Add the remaining ingredients, stir and heat thoroughly for about 3-4 minutes over a low heat. Season and remove from heat. You can warm this for service for the Hoisin Lamb and store the remainder in fridge for future use. There are many other uses for the Chutney as a side to a cheese plate, as a savory sweet sandwich spread or with the Pork in lieu of the peanut sauce.

Wild Striped Bass with Roasted Garlic Butter & Veggies
Yields about 3/ 5 oz portions of fish plus all the fixin's

Ingredients:
1lb Fresh Wild Striped Bass (skin on or off, your choice)
8 oz French green beans (Yellow color if they have them, if not just make it work with the green)
9 each grape tomatoes or 5 cherry tomatoes cut in half
1 cup oven roasted or sautéed mushrooms (pg. 97)
$\frac{1}{2}$ lb roasted Brussels sprouts (pg. 98)
$\frac{3}{4}$ cups cooked apple wood bacon cut into small strips or lardons
3 Tbsp Roasted Garlic Butter (pg. 97)

kosher salt and black pepper
Extra Virgin Olive Oil

Method:
Trim the fish, check for pin bones and cut into (3) 5 oz portions. Generously season both sides with salt and pepper. Heat skillet to high heat and place a splash of olive oil. Sear the fish starting with the skin side down (if skin on fish) and cook for about 2 minutes, then flip over and cook for about another 1-2 minutes. Do not overcook. Set aside until all of your other ingredients are ready.
In a separate skillet, heat to high heat and add a splash of oil. Add the tomatoes, blanched green beans, some salt and pepper and sauté briefly until tomatoes begin to burst and get some color, then add the cooked bacon, roasted mushrooms & roasted Brussels sprouts. Heat everything through. Do not overcook the mixture since the ingredients have been pre-roasted/cooked; simply heat through.
In a fish pan, add the roasted garlic butter. To finish the cooking process, heat the fish on low heat for about 3 more

Wild Striped Bass with Roasted Garlic Butter & Veggies, continued:

minutes covered on stove top or place in 400 degree oven for about the same amount of time until the fish is cooked through and then let rest while you plate the veggie medley. Place the sautéed veggie/bacon mixture down on the plate, then top with the pieces of fish and drizzle everything with the remaining roasted garlic butter from the pan. You can heat some additional butter in another pan or sauté your veggies with some as well.

Roasted Garlic Butter (for Wild Striped Bass)
Yields 8 oz of butter which can be used for bread or other applications

Ingredients:
8 oz unsalted butter, room temp
$\frac{3}{4}$ Tbsp fire roasted garlic
$\frac{1}{2}$ Tbsp kosher salt
$\frac{1}{2}$ Tbsp ground black pepper
$\frac{1}{2}$ tsp nutmeg

Method:
Blend butter and all ingredients together in a food processor/mixer with a paddle to make a whipped seasoned spread and then chill for future use.

Roasted Mushrooms (for Wild Striped Bass)
Yields about 2 cups of roasted mushrooms

Ingredients:
4 cups cremini mushrooms with stems, thinly sliced
2 Tbsp EVOO

Roasted Mushrooms, continued:

1 tsp kosher salt and pinch of black pepper

Method:
Pre-heat oven to 350 degrees. On a sheet pan/baking sheet, drizzle mushrooms with EVOO, salt and pepper and mix all ingredients together. Bake until mushrooms are caramelized/browned for about 10-15 minutes. Remove and add to veggie medley for striped bass or gobble them up by themselves.

Roasted Brussels Sprouts (for Wild Striped Bass)
Yields about 1 ½ -2 cups of cooked sprouts

Ingredients:
½ lb Brussels sprouts, trimmed and halved
2-3 Tbsp olive oil
kosher salt
black pepper

Method:
Preheat oven to 350 degrees. Mix the Brussels sprouts with the oil, salt and pepper and place them face down on the baking sheet. Roast in the oven until the vegetables are cooked through and golden brown which should take about 10-15 minutes. You can turn them over once during the cooking process or just brown one side. Remove the vegetables from the oven and add to the veggie mixture for the striped bass or like the mushrooms, gobble them up hot out of the oven.

Stuffed Pork Tenderloin
Yields 4-6 portions as an entrée

Ingredients:
1 each 1 ½ - 2 lb Pork Tenderloin (cleaned, excess fat removed)

Stuffing:
4 oz goat cheese (domestic is fine)
2 oz dried figs (any variety)
¼ tsp ground cinnamon
¼ tsp ground black pepper

Method:
Blend all ingredients in food processor until combined and set aside.

Kosher salt
Ground black pepper
Butchers twine (to tie up the loins after stuffing)
Extra virgin olive oil

Method:
Using a boning knife, cut the pork loin by holding the knife at an angle and in a spiral fashion "unroll" the meat by slicing thinly lengthwise and continuously along the side. You will be working your way to the center of the loin and will be cutting one continuous strip of meat until there is none left to cut. Cut as thinly as possible. If desired, use a meat pounder to make the resulting pork roll into a thinner slab. When done, the result will be a thin, rectangular slab of pork which you will be able to fill with stuffing and roll up jelly-roll style. You can also simply fill the middle and roll it up to have just the center filled versus the jelly roll method. Sprinkle kosher salt and pepper on the inside and exterior of the pork loin.

Stuffed Pork Tenderloin, continued:

Place the pork on a flat surface and pat the filling out, spreading it over top (this will be the inside) of the entire surface of the pork. Take one of the short ends and begin rolling this edge toward the center, a little bit at a time, continuing to roll up (jelly-roll style) until the pork loin is log shaped, with a stuffing spiral on each end. Using butchers twine, tie up the loin to secure all of the filling and don't forget to remove the string prior to serving.

Pre-heat oven to 350°F. In a hot pan over high heat, pour a small amount of olive oil into the pan and then sear all sides of the seasoned tenderloin. Finish in pre-heated oven at 350°F for 15-20 minutes covered with foil to avoid drying out the pork. Internal temperature should read 150-155 degrees (pork will continue to cook while resting). Remove from oven and let it rest covered to retain moisture until serving. Cut off butchers twine and then slice loin into medallions. Finish with my Tangy Shallot, White Wine & Mustard Sauce or my Apple Shallot Brandy Glaze from book one. The Currant, Cilantro & Almond Couscous from Side Kicks is a natural fit for this dish.

Grilled Chicken Burger
Yields 8 (6 oz) chicken burgers

Ingredients:
3 lbs ground chicken (I prefer the Perdue brand)
1 Tbsp black pepper
1 Tbsp onion powder
1 Tbsp garlic powder
1.5 tsp ground oregano
2 Tbsp kosher salt
1 Tbsp Tabasco
2 Tbsp fresh thyme

White wine
Extra virgin olive oil

Method:
Place all of the ingredients into a large mixing bowl and blend together. Grab (with your clean hands) about 6 oz, form into a ball, then into a patty and place to the side. The burger is pretty lean so you can use a little olive oil on it when you are grilling. Alternatively, you pan sear it- add some oil to the pan and finish it with a splash of white wine to add a blast of flavor along with some moisture. Put on your favorite bun with all the trimmings or try it with my Sweet & Sour Pickles & Spicy Sweet Honey Mustard.

**in both the turkey and chicken burgers, all of your seasonings are in the mix so there is no need to add more kosher salt or pepper when you cook them off.

Tasty Turkey Burger
Yields 4 (8 oz) turkey burgers

Ingredients:
2 lbs fresh ground turkey (85/15 blend)
$\frac{1}{2}$ Tbsp cumin powder
$\frac{1}{2}$ Tbsp onion powder
$\frac{1}{2}$ Tbsp Worcestershire sauce
1 Tbsp fresh sage, chopped
$\frac{1}{4}$ Tbsp black pepper
1 1/3 Tbsp kosher salt
1 Tbsp olive oil

White wine
Extra virgin olive oil

Method:
Thoroughly blend all of the ingredients in a large mixing bowl by hand (clean hands that is), form into an 8 oz ball and flatten into a patty. Store the burgers covered with plastic wrap in the fridge or you can grill them off immediately like the Chicken Burger using a little bit of olive oil to keep the lean meat from sticking to the grill. You can also pan sear the burgers and finish with a splash of white wine for flavor and moisture. Put on your favorite bun with all the trimmings or try it with my Tzaztiki Sauce or Triple Olive Tapenade.

Guilty Pleasures...

Sweets, chocolates, desserts, candies & treats. Bring 'em on. I love everything sweet and I think it has a lot to do with my Mom-Pat, Thanks Mom ☺ . She loves chocolate more than life and it's a vice for her and always has been. I remember growing up and buying her a 10 lb Hershey's Chocolate Bar for Christmas one year and you know what, she actually ate the whole thing. During the holidays, we never had just pumpkin pie for Thanksgiving. We had that and maybe 5-6 other cookies, cakes and other homemade treats. Our dessert buffets were always as large as or larger than the rest of our holiday meals and you know that I am good with that. A true meal for me is never complete without a bite or a nibble of something sweet or chocolaty. So, if that's how you feel about desserts than this section will give you some new treats to add to your personal list of Guilty Pleasures.

You can get a glimpse of the mini version of my Lemon Vanilla Sponge Cake on the back of this book. The Sponge cake is like what you would see in a Twinkie. I add a little lemon zest and then dress it up with some Mascarpone Cream and Seasonal Berries for a treat that beats that old school shortcake or plain, boring angel food cake any day. The cake is very light and delicate while not being too hard on the waistline unless you smother it in the Mascarpone Cream.

I LOVE BUTTERSCOTH, seriously I do. This pudding is so easy to make and you can serve it warm right out of the oven which is even tastier if you are a warm pudding or custard fan. I use the butterscotch chips that you find at the grocery and I love to finish it with a little salted whipped cream and Nutmeg Walnuts or Cashews to give it a little crunch. I'm craving some right now just writing about it, yum.

The Death by Cocoa Cake is actually a recipe from my good friend Shauna's mom, Jan. The first time she served me a piece of this cake I think I ate 4 more slices...it's sooo addictive. I love the rich creaminess of the cake that comes from the cocoa and buttermilk. I like this cocoa based cake versus a traditional chocolate cake because it has a slightly different flavor along with a rich velvety texture thanks to the addition of our good friend, butter. The cake and the frosting both have two steps but the time it takes to make this cake will be appreciated by your guests and family. This is wonderful on its own or served with my Crème Fraiche Ice Cream. You can pop it in the microwave for a few seconds and you have this warm, gooey, rich and deadly Cocoa Cake.

What's unique about the Roasted Pistachio Oil & White Chocolate Biscotti is that we use the pistachio oil as the fat for the cookie with just a tad of butter. I created this recipe for La Tourangelle Oils and wanted to show other ways to work with their wonderfully handcrafted artisanal oils. If you aren't a biscotti fan because of the crunch, you can bake these once and serve them as a softer cookie. You can also drizzle them with some melted white chocolate if you want to dress them up a bit more. Add a shot of espresso and you will be ready to take on any challenge the day has to offer.

The Crème Fraiche Ice Cream is such a nice change from the standard vanilla. The tanginess of the crème fraiche makes this ice cream really stand out in flavor, not to mention the extra creaminess you get from the crème fraiche itself. You can make this in your home ice cream machine and then sit back and enjoy the compliments. I wanted to share my Hot Fudge and Caramel Sauce recipes with you too, so that you can make delicious sundaes at home. The Caramel Sauce takes some technique and may be the most difficult recipe in the book since making caramel is a true art and adding the ingredients to the sugar base at the right time is key to its success. If you are a marshmallow fan but have never had fresh or Homemade Marshmallow then please make this recipe immediately.

These are so fluffy and airy they blow those yucky little 'Peeps' out of the water. Try these Marshmallows on a smore and you just might cry yourself to sleep by the campfire from being so happy. You can also add your favorite flavor or food coloring to the marshmallows batter and make your own colored, flavored 'Peeps' at home.

Lemon Vanilla Sponge Cake
Yields 24 each-2 layer/2 inch mini shortcakes or
10 each-2 layer/3 inch shortcakes

Ingredients:
8 each large eggs, separated into whites and yolks
8 oz granulated sugar
8 oz all purpose flour, SIFTED
1 ½ oz, unsalted butter, melted and cooled off

1 ½ tsp vanilla extract
3 Tbsp lemon zest

Unsalted butter or pan spray
Ring cutter for cutting out small shortcakes
Powdered sugar for decorating

Method:
In separate mixing bowls, mix half of the sugar with egg yolks
and half of the sugar with egg whites. Beat the yolks until
light yellow and fluffy. Beat the whites to a soft peak stage,
but make sure that when you go to beat the whites, you rinse
off the whisk or the fats from the yolks (the yolks will keep
the whites from going to the soft peak stage). Slowly,add the
sifted flour to egg yolks and sugar (this can get kind of
clumpy), then gently fold the egg whites into the mix and pour
in the melted butter. Grease your sheet tray/baking sheet and
bake at 325 degrees for 5-10 minutes until cake springs back
to the touch. DO not over bake or cake will be very dry and
under-baking will make for a sticky cake since it is a sponge
style cake with very little fat. Once the cake has cooled, I use
my 2 or 3 inch ring cutter by ATECO and cut out individual
little cakes (see picture on the back cover) and set them to
the side. You will layer the cakes with sliced berries and

106

Lemon Vanilla Sponge Cake, continued:

Whipped Mascarpone Cream and you can garnish with some fresh mint. I like to sprinkle a little powdered sugar on them which makes them look nicer. I normally do two layers which are enough, but you could go higher. You can also do a sheet style cake, and then you would not have to cut out the miniature sponge cakes. Just spread the Mascarpone Cream, layer the berries and then cut slices for your guests.

** soft peak stage- think of the droopy mountain where the Grinch lives, a soft peak where it has some shape/structure but is not stiff.

Strawberries for Sponge Cake
**you can use whatever berry is in season to make your favorite shortcake (black, blue or raspberry)

Ingredients:
8 oz strawberries, thinly sliced
2 Tbsp of sugar

Method:
Pour sugar over strawberries, mix together gently with a fork or spoon and serve with the sponge cakes and Mascarpone Cream.

Whipped Mascarpone Cream (for Lemon Vanilla Shortcakes)
Yields just over 16 oz of topping

Ingredients:
16 oz mascarpone cheese
2 tsp salt

Whipped Mascarpone Cream, continued:

$\frac{1}{4}$ cup granulated sugar
1 $\frac{1}{4}$ cups heavy cream
$\frac{1}{2}$ Tbsp vanilla extract

Method:
Add all ingredients in a bowl under a stand mixer and whip with whisk attachment until light and fluffy. Do not over whip or it will become BUTTER.

Butterscotch Pudding
Yields 10-12 (4 oz portions)

Ingredients:
24 oz whole milk
9oz heavy cream
3 large eggs
6 large egg yolks
6 oz granulated sugar
12 oz butterscotch chips

Method:
Scald milk and cream over high heat and remove from the stovetop. Whisk together the eggs and sugar until completely blended, then slowly pour small amounts of hot cream/milk mixture into eggs while whisking (don't go too fast or you will have scrambled eggs). Quickly add the chips and whisk until melted. Strain through fine sieve and pour the mixture into 4 oz ramekins or small baking dishes. Place the ramekins in a shallow baking dish and place into 300-325 degree oven. Once in the oven, pour water around the ramekins (water bath) and bake for about 45-60 minutes. Keep checking to see that the custard has set, remove from the oven and water bath and let cool. Cover with plastic wrap otherwise they will form a skin on the top (if you like a pudding skin then leave uncovered for storage). Garnish with whipped cream, mint and your favorite brittle or my Nutmeg Walnuts or Cashews.

Death by Cocoa Cake
Yields enough cake for a small army
** this cake has 2 parts for the cake and the frosting, please read the recipe at least once before getting started, it will save you some headaches...trust me!

Ingredients: (Cake)
Part I
3 cups granulated sugar
3 cups all purpose flour
3 each large eggs (beaten)
$1\frac{1}{2}$ cups buttermilk
1 Tbsp baking soda
1 Tbsp vanilla extract
$\frac{1}{2}$ Tbsp kosher salt

Part II
$\frac{3}{4}$ lbs unsalted sweet cream butter
6 Tbsp Hershey's American Processed Cocoa powder
$1\frac{1}{2}$ cups cold water

Method:
In a large bowl, mix all ingredients together from part I of the recipe and set aside. Either in the microwave or on the stovetop, bring part II to a boil and whisk together completely. Add part II into part I and mix all together in a mixer, do not overwork. Pour cakes into an ungreased $9\frac{1}{2}$ x 13 baking pan (or other large similar size pan) and bake in a pre-heated oven at 400 degrees for about 25 minutes, check for doneness. Make sure you have the icing prepared as you will frost the cake while it is warm.

Death by Cocoa Cake, continued:

Ingredients: (Icing)
Part I
3 oz unsalted sweet cream butter
3 Tbsp Hershey's American processed cocoa powder
1/3 cups heavy cream

Part II
$\frac{3}{4}$ lbs powdered sugar (sifted)
$\frac{1}{2}$ tsp vanilla extract
$\frac{1}{2}$ tsp kosher salt

Method:
Bring the ingredients of part I to a boil via stovetop or microwave. Pour this over the sifted powdered sugar, vanilla and salt, mix completely and pour over cake once removed from the oven. Let sit unless you can't wait to eat it warm. Seriously, you can eat this cake at room temperature or it is really delicious if you warm the slices at service and serve them with my Crème Fraiche Ice Cream or whipped cream.

Roasted Pistachio Oil & White Chocolate Biscotti
Yields about 30-36 biscotti cookies

Ingredients:
½ cup Toasted Pistachios, salted or unsalted- rolled in flour
½ cup White Chocolate Chips
3 Tbsp Roasted Pistachio Oil, La Tourangelle brand
2 Tbsp Unsalted Butter, room temperature
1 cup Sugar
½ Tbsp Baking Powder
¼ tsp kosher salt
2 Large Eggs
2 cups All Purpose Flour (plus a Tbsp for the pistachios)
½ Tbsp Vanilla Extract
1 Tbsp Lemon Zest

Method:
In a blender or food processor mix the sugar, Pistachio oil and butter. Gradually add the eggs and blend, then gradually add the flour, baking powder and kosher salt. Take the toasted pistachios and roll them in a pinch of flour. Now mix in the lemon zest, vanilla, white chocolate chips & floured pistachios and blend for another minute or two until the dough is brought together. You may have to work it with your hands to bring it all together into a ball of dough with the nuts and chips. Form it into four equal size logs of dough and place into the refrigerator wrapped in saran wrap for at least an hour.
Heat your oven to 350 degrees and then place the dough logs onto greased cookie sheets and leave them some space to spread out and bake for 20-25 minutes until golden brown. Remove them from the oven once browned and let cool slightly.

Roasted Pistachio Oil & Chocolate Biscotti, continued:

Carefully move the cooled, baked logs onto a cutting board and slice into ½ inch diagonal slices while still warm. Using a spatula, pick up the delicate slices and place them back on the baking sheet and bake for another 5-10 minutes. Remove from oven and cool. Store in an air-tight container for up to one week.

**ps you can use other nut oils like walnut, hazelnut or pumpkin if you can't find the pistachio

Crème Fraiche Ice Cream
Yields 1 quart of ice cream

Ingredients:
3 cups half & half
1 cup heavy cream
1 ¼ cups granulated sugar
12 large egg yolks
2 tsp kosher salt
2 tsp vanilla extract

1 cup crème fraiche (added half way during the ice cream maker process)

Method:
Place half & half, cream and sugar into a deep pan/stockpot. Bring to a simmer over medium heat while whisking and heat until you see small bubbles around the side and the sugar is dissolved. Remove from heat. In a large mixing bowl beat the eggs. Using the heated cream/sugar mixture, temper the eggs by gradually whisking 1/2 cup of the hot liquid into the yolks (Liason). Continue this process until everything is integrated and then whisk all together. Place back onto low heat and heat slowly as to not cook the eggs but to thicken the mixture to cover the back of a spoon (nappe'). Remove this from the heat and chill in preparation for putting into your home ice cream maker. Once completely chilled, pour into your ice cream maker and start churning away. About 15 minutes into the process add your cold crème fraiche and let it finish processing. Place ice cream into freezer if not using right away, otherwise scoop it up and serve with a warm slice of Death by Cocoa Cake or use for a sundae with my Hot Fudge and Caramel Sauces.

Hot Fudge Sauce
Yields about 2 cups of delicious hot fudge

Ingredients:
8 oz unsweetened chocolate
4 Tbsp butter
1 1/3 cup boiling water
2 cups sugar
$\frac{1}{4}$ cup corn syrup
$\frac{1}{4}$ cup semi-sweet chocolate chips
$\frac{1}{2}$ tsp vanilla
$\frac{1}{2}$ tsp salt
$\frac{1}{2}$ cup heavy cream

Method:
Heat water to a boil, add all of other ingredients and bring to a boil stirring constantly. Whisk together over medium heat until the chocolate sauce begins to thicken and it coats the back of a spoon. Remove from heat and serve. I love adding this to vanilla ice cream and malt powder and making a Hot Fudge Malt- try it if you've never done it. It makes for pure insanity and so much better than an old school chocolate malt.

Caramel Sauce

Yields about 2 cups of caramel sauce

**this recipe is tricky as there is a true art to making caramel, so if you are worried about trying it then make a smaller batch until you get the technique down and take your time.

Ingredients:

1 ½ cups granulated sugar
½ cup water
1 ¼ cups heavy cream
½ tsp vanilla extract

Method:

Mix the water and sugar together using your CLEAN FINGERS in a medium heavy-bottomed saucepan with no heat on. Cook mixture over low heat for 5 to 10 minutes, until the sugar dissolves. DO NOT STIR. Increase the heat to medium and boil uncovered until the sugar turns a warm chestnut brown- about 20-30 minutes, gently swirling the pan to stir the mixture. Be careful – the mixture is extremely hot! Watch the mixture very carefully towards the end, as it will go from caramel to burnt very quickly. Turn off the heat. Stand back to avoid splattering while you slowly add the heavy cream and vanilla. Don't worry - the cream will bubble violently and the caramel will solidify if you have done it all properly.

If you added your cream and vanilla too early, you can attempt to save it by simmering over low heat, stirring constantly until the caramel dissolves and the sauce is smooth, about 2 minutes. Allow to cool to room temperature and the sauce will thicken as it sits. Serve this over the Crème Fraiche Ice Cream.

Homemade Marshmallows

Yields about

** this recipe is a 3-step process, so take your time and read over the recipe once or twice before you try to tackle it the first time.

Ingredients:

I.
$\frac{3}{4}$ oz powdered gelatin
6 fl oz cold water

II.
6 fl oz water
2 cups sugar
$\frac{3}{4}$ cup light corn syrup

III.
$\frac{1}{4}$ cup light corn syrup
1 Tbsp vanilla extract

Method:

Add the gelatin and water (I.) to a small bowl and set aside to allow the gelatin to bloom/activate. Cook the 2nd set (II.) of water, sugar and corn syrup on the stove top in a medium sauce pan to 240 degrees on a candy thermometer. Once it hits 240 degrees, add the other corn syrup and vanilla (III.) and pour the hot mixture into the gelatin that has bloomed. Put all ingredients into a mixer and whip for about 10 minutes until the mixture becomes light and fluffy. Spread the marshmallow batter into a baking pan with pan spray and waxed paper and then more spray to let it set.

Homemade Marshmallows, continued:

Once the marshmallow has set, cut into small $\frac{1}{2}$ inch marshmallows or whatever size you fancy. Make your own homemade Rocky Road Sundae using my Crème Fraiche Ice Cream, Hot Fudge and Caramel Sauces and the Nutmeg Walnuts.

More Cocktails, Please...

You can ask any of my life- long friends or colleagues in the restaurant business and they will assure you that I have always been one to make a mean drink or tasty cocktail. My philosophy on the alcoholic beverage has always been to make them good and to make them strong using premium liquors/liqueurs along with the freshest ingredients and fresh squeezed juices. I have put together a sampling of a few drinks that I have created over the last couple years and served at several restaurants as well as cooking and cocktail parties here in NYC. None of them are too crazy or complicated to make. It's all about less is more; too many ingredients in my food or drinks have never worked for me. If you look at the two Bloody Mary recipes, you will see that they have a lot of the same ingredients but one difference is the fresh Yellow Tomato in one version. A bloody mary is all about the balance of savory and salty with a little bit of heat, making sure the flavor of the tomato doesn't get lost in the shuffle. The red chili garlic sauce is my secret ingredient along with the celery seed and salts. Have fun with your garnish on these and use things like roasted asparagus, my Sweet & Sour Pickles or pickled jalapenos if you're looking for more heat.

Both the Ginger POM Martini and The 'Apple Jack' were created for a holiday cooking party last year for The Culinary Loft in SoHo, where I have been doing classes and workshops for the past 3 years. The warmth of The 'Apple Jack' is perfect for a cold snowy evening and if the heat of the drink doesn't lend a hand then good old Jack, (Daniels that is) will. Both of these drinks have flavored simple syrup that help to give them a boost of sweetness and extra flavor. The sparkle of the ginger ale is a nice pep for the Ginger POM Martini and the fresh apple cider is key to the success of The 'Apple Jack'.

The Guava Mojito and Prickly Pear Margarita were both served at Crave on 42nd in NYC. I love a great margarita and the tartness of the Prickly Pear Puree (from Perfect Puree of Napa Valley- see the front of my book for Where to Buy) is what makes this drink so fantastic, not to mention the beautiful natural magenta color from the prickly pear. The drink is tangy and strong with the right balance of fresh lemon and lime. It is so refreshing that you will want more than one so as long as you aren't the designated driver, feel free to indulge. The 10 Cane Rum, fresh mint, lime and Guava nectar breathe new life into the over exposed Mojito. There is something sexy about muddled drinks that people really love so by giving it your all to mash/muddle your mint and lime together , you'll get your guest (s) attention and they'll be lining up to find out what you're creating at the bar.

Let's talk about The Brooklyn Blues. I love Brooklyn and it does not give me the blues but since I used Blueberry and Pom juices I had to get the blues in there somewhere. If you haven't tried the new Absolut Brooklyn, you need to try it, as its red apple and ginger flavors work so well together. Spike Lee actually did the artwork for the bottle which is real cool and this is truly one of the more unique flavored vodkas that I've tasted in awhile. These drinks go down way too easy; I created this drink this past summer in Vermont on a summer excursion with the Girvin Family, fun times for all and too fun for some .

**cocktails are great to enjoy but please drink responsibly and please do not drink and drive

120

Traditional Bloody Mary Mix
Yields 6 drinks using (8 oz of mix)

Ingredients for your Mix:
1 each /46 oz can of your favorite tomato juice
1 oz Worcestershire sauce
1 oz Tabasco sauce
1 $\frac{1}{4}$ Tbsp horseradish
$\frac{1}{2}$ tsp kosher salt
1 $\frac{1}{4}$ Tbsp black pepper
1 $\frac{1}{4}$ oz fresh lemon juice
1 $\frac{1}{4}$ oz red chili garlic sauce (The Rooster)
1 $\frac{1}{4}$ oz granulated sugar
1 $\frac{1}{4}$ tsp celery seed
1 $\frac{1}{4}$ tsp celery salt

Cocktail:
4 oz of your favorite Premium Vodka (I like 'em strong- use less based on your tolerance level)
6-8 oz Bloody Mary Mix (from mixture above)

Roasted Asparagus Spears
Sweet & Sour Pickles (pg. 43)
Lemon and limes
Kosher salt
Martini Shaker
Pint glass
Ice

Method:
Mix all of the Bloody Mary Mix ingredients together in a pitcher, stir and let chill. Dip glass rim into fresh lime juice and coat with kosher salt -then set to the side.

Traditional Bloody Mary Mix, continued:

Blend your vodka and Mix ingredients together from the cocktail portion in a shaker and shake like crazy or stir until everything is incorporated completely and serve over ice in a tall pint glass. Garnish drink with roasted asparagus, Sweet & Sour Pickles, lemon and lime wedges.

Yellow Tomato Mary
Yields 6 drinks using (8 oz of mix)

Ingredients for your Mix:
8 each yellow beefsteak tomatoes (cored and chopped into 4)-
yields about ½ gallon of puree
1 oz Chipotle Tabasco
1 oz Worcestershire sauce
1 ¼ Tbsp horseradish
1 ¼ oz fresh lemon juice
1 ¼ oz red chili garlic sauce (The Rooster)
1 ¼ oz granulated sugar
1 ¼ Tbsp celery seed
1 ¼ Tbsp celery salt
½ tsp black pepper
1 ¼ tsp kosher salt

Cocktail:
4 oz of your favorite Premium Vodka (I like 'em strong- use
less based on your tolerance level)
6-8 oz Yellow Tomato Bloody Mary Mix

Asparagus
Sweet & Sour Pickles (pg.43)
Lemon and limes
Kosher salt
Martini Shaker
Pint glass
Ice

Method:
Core all tomatoes, cut in 4 pieces and blend in a food
processor/blender. Add all of the ingredients together and

Yellow Tomato Mary, continued:

taste for seasoning, then put into your pitcher, stir and let chill. Dip glass rim into fresh lime juice and coat with kosher salt; set to the side. Blend your vodka and mix ingredients in a shaker and shake like crazy or stir until everything is incorporated completely and serve over ice in a tall pint glass. Garnish drink with roasted asparagus, Sweet & Sour Pickles, lemon and lime wedges. With the use of the fresh tomatoes and chipotle Tabasco this has a unique flavor all its own, although the composition of ingredients is similar to the Traditional Bloody Mary Mix.

Ginger POM Martini
Yields 1 martini

Ingredients:
1 oz ginger simple syrup (see below)
2 oz premium vodka
3 oz ginger ale
2 oz POM juice (pomegranate juice)
1 Tbsp fresh lime juice
ginger and sugar dust for garnish (see below)

ginger syrup:
½ cup granulated sugar
½ cup water
½ tsp ginger powder
Syrup method:
In a small sauce pan, heat all ingredients over high heat until sugar is dissolved. You can cook for a couple minutes which will thicken the syrup, the choice is yours.

ginger/sugar dust:
½ cup granulated sugar
½ tsp ginger powder
Ginger dust method:
Stir the sugar and ginger powder and mix thoroughly. Set aside in a dry place.

Chilled Martini Glass
Martini Shaker
Lime juice
Ice

Ginger POM Martini, continued:

Method:
Make your ginger syrup and ginger dust in advance. Dip your chilled martini glass rim in lime juice and then dip in ginger/sugar dust. Measure & blend all of your cockatil ingredients in a martini shaker with ice, shake wildly and serve in chilled and garnished martini glass.

The 'Apple Jack'
Yields 1 mug of goodness

Ingredients:
4 oz fresh apple cider
1 oz cinnamon & nutmeg simple syrup (see below)
2 oz Jack Daniels
squeeze of fresh lemon
cinnamon sticks for garnish
slices of red apple for garnish, sliced into discs

cinnamon syrup:
$\frac{1}{2}$ cup granulated sugar
$\frac{1}{2}$ cup water
$\frac{1}{4}$ tsp cinnamon
$\frac{1}{4}$ tsp nutmeg

Syrup method:
In a small sauce pan, heat all ingredients over high heat until sugar is dissolved. You can cook for a couple minutes which will thicken the syrup, the longer you cook the thicker the syrup.

Drink Method:
Heat the apple cider on the stove top with simple syrup. Add to a coffee mug with Jack Daniels and a squeeze of lemon. Slice red apple into a thin disk and float on top of warmed beverage along with cinnamon stick. Warms you up on those cold winter days--thanks Jack.

Guava Mojito
Yields 1 mojito

Ingredients:
1 ½ ounces of 10 Cane Rum
8 mint leaves
2 limes, sliced
2 ounces of guava nectar/puree
1 ounce simple syrup (use the method for the syrups from Ginger POM or The Apple Jack just using ½ cup water and ½ cup granulated sugar cooked down on the stovetop without any other flavors/spices)
Splash of soda

Pint glass
Muddling Stick
Martini Shaker
Wine Glass
Ice

Method:
In a pint glass add the mint and limes and muddle/mash them together. Pour the rum, guava and syrup (NOT the soda) into a martini shaker & shake all ingredients together feverishly. Pour over ice in a wine glass and top off with a splash of soda.

Muddle- is to combine ingredients, usually in the bottom of a mixing glass, by pressing them with a muddler (bartenders' tool like a pestle) before adding the majority of the liquid ingredients.

Prickly Pear Margarita
Yields 1 perfect margarita

Ingredients:
1 ½ oz of Tequila (I usually use Patron Silver)
2 oz Prickly Pear Perfect Puree (from perfectpuree.com)
1 oz Cointreau (you can also use Grand Marnier or Orange Liqueur)
2 oz fresh lemon and lime juices

1 cup of Ice
Fresh lime slices
Kosher Salt or cocktail salt for rim
Bucket Glass or Margarita Glass
Cocktail shaker or Electric Blender

Method:
Add all ingredients plus ice into cocktail shaker and shake like crazy, then pour into salted bucket glass and garnish with slice of fresh lime. Enjoy.

Blended Method:
Add all ingredients into electric blender along with 1 cup of ice and blend until foamy and slushy. Pour into salted margarita glass and garnish with slice of fresh lime. Drink Up.

Salted Rim:
Dip mouth/rim of bucket glass or margarita glass into fresh lime juice then place in kosher salt on a flat plate.

The Brooklyn Blues
Yields 1 cocktail
**Absolut Brooklyn is a delicious mix of red apple & ginger...
yummy!

Ingredients:
3 oz Absolut Brooklyn Vodka
6 oz POM Blueberry Juice (pomegranate & blueberry)
 2 oz ginger ale

Bucket glass
Ice

Method:
Throw your ice into the bucket glass and stir with Absolut
Brooklyn and POM blueberry juice. Top with the ginger ale and
give another stir. You have a cocktail that it is way too easy to
make and way too easy to drink. The bonus, it's full of
antioxidants.

About the Author

Dave's road into the culinary world was far from traditional. After leaving a successful career and company in the technology industry behind, Dave chose to pursue his real love and passion-cooking and making people smile through his food. He headed back to school and graduated with honors from the Le Cordon Bleu in Pasadena, California. Halfway through the program, he formed his own catering company and took on the Executive Chef role at 'XO Wine Bistro' in Manhattan Beach, CA. He soon built a strong local following of customers that enjoyed his multi-regional cuisine that ranged from Southern Barbecue to SouthEast Asian and beyond.

Dave was a Cheftestant on the first season of Bravo's *Top Chef*. Fans will never forget his famous Black Truffle Mac n' Cheese and, of course, Dave's success in making it to the finals in competition. After appearing on *Top Chef*, Dave made the leap to New York City and was an Executive/Consulting Chef at Lola, Crave on 42nd, and VYNL Restaurants. Additionally, Dave began building relationships with the University of Illinois (Champaign-Urbana), The Culinary Loft in Soho, The French Culinary Institute, In Good Taste-Portland, Oregon, Cisco Systems, Perfect Puree and many more.

In expanding his new business model, Dave has been working hard to keep his name and most importantly his food out there for the public. Since the release of *Flavor Quest, Volume 1* in 2009, he has been focused on promoting his book and working on lots of exciting projects. Currently, Chef Dave travels around the country for various Food & Wine Festivals, winemaker dinners, consulting projects, corporate and private catering events along with numerous guest chef and pop-up restaurant appearances.

In 2010, he started teaching classes in American Regional Cuisine at The French Culinary Institute for their Recreational Division with more classes slated for 2011. Dave continues to teach at The Culinary Loft for Executives from MTV, Oracle, NBC and other large corporations. Chef Dave supports several charitable organizations including the Make-A-Wish Foundation, The American Heart Association, Ronald McDonald House (NYC), Share Our Strength, Leake & Watts, Greenwich House ,Share our Strength (Taste of the Nation) and The Special Olympics.

Index

Index, continued:

Index, continued:

LaVergne, TN USA
23 January 2011
213618LV00003B/171/P